Graw-Hill Paperbacks

>>$6.95

HOW TO COMMUNICATE

THE MANNING SELVAGE & LEE GUIDE TO CLEAR WRITING AND SPEECH

CHARLES EINSTEIN

How to
COMMUNICATE

The Manning, Selvage
& Lee Guide to
Clear Writing and Speech

How to
COMMUNICATE

CHARLES EINSTEIN

McGRAW-HILL BOOK COMPANY

New York St. Louis San Francisco Bogotá Guatemala
Hamburg Lisbon Madrid Mexico Montreal Panama Paris
San Juan São Paulo Tokyo Toronto

ISBN 0-07-039928-X

1 2 3 4 5 6 7 8 9 F G R F G R 8 7 6 5

LIBRARY OF CONGRESS CATALOGING IN PUBLICATION DATA

Einstein, Charles.
How to communicate.
1. English language—Usage—Dictionaries.
I. Manning, Selvage & Lee.   II. Title.
PE1628.E35 1984   428'.00973   84-23346
ISBN 0-07-039928-X

Book design by Patrice Fodero

ACKNOWLEDGMENTS

Many colleagues and friends helped shape this book, and I want particularly to acknowledge the assistance and counsel of Bob Begam, Ellen Campbell, Bob Creamer, Tony D'Antonio, Joanne Dolinar, Joan Eckerman, Peter Griffin, Lee Hays, Dorrie Ignatovich, Al and Iris MacCarthy, Tim McGinnis, Bill Pearsall, Arthur Pincus, Martin Remnitz, Ray Robinson, Peter Schwed, Sam Seidel, Al Silverman, George Simko, Dan Weaver, and Luis Zea.

C. E.

CONTENTS

PART 1

Preamble   1

PART 2

Glossary   45

Part 1

PREAMBLE

The Ears Have It

This book is an outgrowth of two recessions. The economic recession of 1982 was one of them. The other drew emphasis that same year from a report by the National Education Commission showing the United States had gone from 18th to 49th among the literate nations of the world. Today nearly 25 million Americans are functionally illiterate. Millions more are "aliterate": they can read and write, but they don't.

In many countries this situation, to whatever extent it exists, is confined chiefly to the undereducated and the foreign-born. In the United States, by contrast, it is found at every level of daily life. "Most people hate to write," Deborah Dumaine, founder of a remedial organization for business executives, has said. "Upper middle managers have all the skills except that one." Or take the series of war games conducted by the U.S. Army in California in the summer of 1983. Our side lost. Prominent among the reasons given for the defeat was the inability of officers to issue understandable commands. "It's a rampant problem," Ms. Dumaine said. Donna Woolfolk Cross, the author of *Word Abuse*, had even stronger words for it: "The loss of coherence is a signature of the time."

Under such circumstances, it is hardly surprising to find people turning more and more to professional communicators. Business was down nearly everywhere in the recession of 1982, but in the public relations industry it was up. While a number of elements have contributed to this growth, the recession in literacy can be considered one of them, and it has been ironical to see this happening in a nation whose technological leadership in the physical science of communication is the envy of the world. "Despite the miracles of the new databases and computer systems," Lewis H. Lapham, the editor of *Harper's*, has written, "we seem to know less than we did when we sealed letters with wax and waited eight months for a reply from London." Leslie Lieber, a former editor at *This Week* magazine, put it another way. "We have more and more wonderful means of saying things," he observed, "and less and less wonderful things to say."

Indeed, there are educators and others who sense that, far from stemming the decline in literacy, the computer may have helped bring it about. The first such machines, introduced more than 40 years ago, were used to score college exams and other tests by "reading" the checkmarks placed by the student in the multiple-choice answer boxes. The ease with which such exams could be machine-graded, in terms of checkmarks instead of written responses, brought a virtual end to the use of such exams as a means of testing respondents' abilities to express themselves. Before long, even the bar exams were mostly multiple-choice. (Written assignments still do exist, at least in some places, but even there the result may be prefabricated. "TERMPAPER CATALOG," an ad in *Playboy* says. "14,278 research papers to choose from—all subjects. Save time and improve your grades.")

Those who resist the trend may be a minority, but they are out there, and at Manning, Selvage & Lee, chairman Robert Schwartz and president Edward Stanton have made skilled, expressive writing a matter of agency-wide priority. Like many among the MS&L staff throughout the United States and the world, their background is journalistic; visitors to the firm's international headquarters in New York have come away mildly disoriented from finding both the chairman and the president working in shirtsleeves with typewriters at their desks. Both served as reporters, writers and editors, Stanton most notably with *Women's Wear Daily* and Schwartz with the old International News Service—two organizations known for good writing. Schwartz in fact dealt daily with an additional factor: unlike its larger rivals, the Associated Press and United Press, the INS had no separate wire service for radio and television stations; the same news report that went to newspapers went to broadcasters too. So the stories had to be written for the ear as well as the eye.

And that is without question the major ingredient in good communicating. Almost all serious linguists and grammarians, from Fowler to Strunk and White, from Campbell to Nunberg, have stressed the sound, rather than the sight, of words. Some words, like *IOU*, aren't words to begin with; the eye simply serves to escort them from the printed page to the ear, where they take their meaning. "When you finish penning a passage of your own, read it to yourself—aloud," Marc Fisher wrote in the preface to his revised edition of Dana W. Niswender's *Horace Mann Handbook of English*. "You'll be surprised how *hearing* what you write can help."

At Manning, Selvage & Lee, this is taken one step farther. The passages are read aloud—but not just by people who wrote them. Once a piece of copy—a news release, say, or the text for a corporate message—has been readied for distribution, it is read simultaneously by two people, one of them reading aloud, the other's eyes following the typescript page. More than just a proofreading exercise (though it serves that purpose too), this gets an added touch: whenever it's practicable, the person reading aloud has never seen the copy before!

It is done this way because even the most experienced writer can slip from time to time, not just on a point of spelling or grammar but on the point of clarity. There is nothing grammatically wrong with *He was the doctor son of a doctor father who won several awards*, and surely the writer knows which of the two—the father or the son—was the award winner. But did the writer let the reader know? *The baron sat between the duke and his secretary*: Whose secretary? The baron's or the duke's?

Reading his own work—even reading it aloud—the original writer is not apt to spot anything wrong with sentences like those; after all, he already knows what they mean. But a stranger might well stop to re-examine the words, and there's the tip-off. In short, if someone unfamiliar with the text can read it aloud without stumbling or pausing in the wrong places, we are pretty safe to believe the piece reads clearly.

The secretmost part of this secret to effective communicating is of course that it is no secret at all. From our earliest years, we learned our language by hearing it: listening to a lullaby, being read to, singing the alphabet song. As adults to this day, we see people moving their lips while reading on the bus or subway, others talking to themselves as they pass us on the street; and if most of us suppress the outward signs, the fact is that all of us do those things. The Greatest Story Ever

Preamble

Told—the Bible—was exactly that: *told*, centuries before anyone put it on paper. Homer was a singer, not a writer. And when writers did appear—Virgil, Milton, Shakespeare—what they wrote was more to be heard than seen. "I do not want actors or actresses to understand my plays," George Bernard Shaw wrote. "That is not necessary. If they will pronounce the correct sounds I can guarantee the results."

We can say here parenthetically that there are grammatical purists who will find instant fault with that last sentence of Shaw's. They'll insist he should have used a comma after *sounds*, pointing to a long-established rule that the comma must be used to separate a dependent from an independent clause. Rule or no rule, they are wrong. The purpose of a comma is to indicate a pause, and by so doing give added clarity to the passage, and Shaw neither needed nor (we must assume) intended a pause at that point.

But English is the champion rogue of languages, and another sentence, structured identically to Shaw's, might not only tolerate the comma but demand it. Look again at Shaw's *If they will only pronounce the correct sounds I can guarantee the results*. Now shape another sentence of the same construction: *If they don't design every last bolt and screw the French make up for it in other ways*. Put a comma after *screw*, and the thing makes sense. Fail to do so and we're left confused, and with good reason: the foremost phrase leaping out at us is *screw the French*.

Another old-time rule is one that President Ronald Reagan recollected from his school days in the message he sent to the 1983 finalists in the National Spelling Bee: "*I* before *E* except after *C*, or when sounded like *A* as in *neighbor* or *weigh*." Either foreign financiers' ancient heirs counterfeit their weirdly heightened seismic seizures, or that too is a rule without an exception.

In brief, if anybody tries to sell you the notion that all you have to do to master the language is memorize a few basic rules, better start counting the spoons. Not only is good writing hard work, but uncommonly so: the more proficient you become, the harder it gets. To choose between the two different ways you know to say something at the age of 18 is one thing; keep at it, and, as your skills improve with time,

6

you realize a generation later there are 20 different ways to say it, making the choice 10 times more difficult. In a book review for *Sports Illustrated*, author Robert W. Creamer wrote, "Bil Gilbert, who has explored jungles, crawled through caves on his belly and written six books, says, 'Writing is probably the most fatiguing thing I know.' " In conversation with a friend afterwards, Creamer said, "I think Gilbert understated the case."

One way out is to take refuge in what William A. Caldwell, columnist for the Bergen County (New Jersey) *Sunday Record*, has described as "the Choctaw called business English: 'Yours of 18th inst. rec'd and contents noted, and in reply would state . . .' The stuff flows, page after page, as deadpan and impenetrable as the testimony of a four-star general with his shirttails afire." William Zinsser, an authority on writing, spent a number of years cataloguing such four-star testimony, mainly for its ability to say nothing. "A generation ago our leaders told us where they stood and what they believed," Zinsser says in his book *On Writing Well*. "Today they perform the most strenuous verbal feats to escape this fate." To one politician, who held four major cabinet positions in the 1970s, went Zinsser's first prize for the most wishy-washy sentence of the decade: "And yet, on balance, affirmative action has, I think, been a qualified success." Surely there was nothing qualified about the politician's success—having won first prize in Zinsser's contest, he also won second prize, for this beaut: "And so, at last, I come to the one firm conviction that I mentioned at the beginning: it is that the subject is too new for final judgments."

Here too, however, those who seek a better way are wrong to look for a quick fix. "What is 'correct' usage?" Zinsser writes. "We have no king to establish the King's English; we only have the President's English—which we don't want." The language does have rules, and reasons for them, but there's more to it than that, and this book is not a rule book. Nor is it a *style* book—not at least in the narrow sense of wanting to assert whether Zinsser was right or wrong in using a capital *P* in *the President's* (though in this case he was right, as he usually is: he capitalized the *P* to balance the capital *K* in the established phrase *King's English*). In general, is it *the President* or *the president*, *the pope* or *the*

Pope? (The Associated Press does it one way, the *Los Angeles Times* the other.) Generations of editors and grammarians have battled over minutiae like that, or whether we should write *traveler* or *traveller*, or what to do about the serial comma. What's a serial comma? It's the last comma in a series. Do we write *the bold, the bad, and the beautiful*, as does *The New Yorker*, or *the bold, the bad and the beautiful*, as does *The New York Times?* One answer to that question—an answer with a good deal to recommend it—comes from *A Dictionary of Contemporary American Usage*, by Bergen and Cornelia Evans: "A sensible person will use this comma or not as he pleases, and will refuse to argue the point with anybody."

Least of all do we need to concern ourselves with such questions if we are writing nonfiction for publication: whatever periodicals or publishing houses we write for will see to it that the stuff conforms to their own in-house rules for style (as McGraw-Hill is doubtless doing with this stuff). More to the point, this book was not designed only for those who write for publication. The hope instead is that it can be at least of some use to anyone seeking to improve the way he or she communicates.

To be sure, a certain consistency in styling is desirable: if you write *the pope* in one sentence, don't make him *the Pope* in the next. But even there, the only real purpose is to avoid giving off a feel of uncertainty in the way you communicate. If you say it aloud, no one will know whether you intended a capital *P* or not, but most communication, even when it is intended to be spoken or even pictured, starts with the written word. Someone once asked movie producer Sam Goldwyn who he thought was the most important figure connected with the making of a film: The director? The actors? The writer? The cameraman? The editor? The composer of the music? The costume or set designers? "The writer," Goldwyn said. "Without him, none of the others has a job."

Goldwyn himself was justly famous for the way he put English to use. Asked what he thought of the atom bomb, he said, "It's dynamite!" On verbal agreements: "They're not worth the paper they're written on." On color television: "I'll believe it when I see it in black and white." Those and other sayings, some of which he actually said, were, if we analyze them, the expressions of an immigrant who grew up with another tongue, then encountered American English and simply took it at face value. Generations of foreigners—Victor Borge, Señor Wences, Chef Tell, Johnny Lee—have made careers in comedy by doing the same thing. But so have uncounted native-born writers, from Mark Twain and Finley Peter Dunne to S. J. Perelman and Peter DeVries. It's a funny language.

A funny language, and a complicated one—which in great part is what makes it funny. We have said that most communication starts with the written word, but when a mother spots her young son halfway up a tree and cries, "Climb down from there!" she is communicating without recourse to a script. She is also demonstrating the complexity of the language. *Climb* means to go up. How can you climb down?

Forget *climb*—what about *down*? There are eight parts of speech in English, and the word *down*, depending on how it is used, can be any one of six of them (noun, verb, adjective, adverb, preposition, interjection). Or take as simple a word as *pitch*. Simple it may be, but Webster's Second International has 55 separate definitions for it. Some words, for that matter, not only have more than one definition, but can mean the precise opposite of themselves. *Sanction* means both to permit or to forbid. *Overlook*, as in *If you overlook the park, you'll have a great view from your room*, can mean either to look at or not to look at. A *suspicious* dealer at the blackjack table may be one who suspects or one who is suspected.

Look up *condescending* in *The Oxford Universal Dictionary*. It means patronizing. Now look up *patronizing*. It means condescending. There is a difference, but no one, not even the dictionaries, can get a real handle on it. Interesting: The perfect squelch, if you think you're being condescended to, is to say, "Don't patronize me!" If you think you're being patronized, you say, "Don't condescend to me!"

A difficult language to control? Consider the following:

This presents us with a choice: to take everyone with a hope and half a story credit into the Guild, whereupon they become members whom (under the best terms we could negotiate with the Department) it would take 10 years before they became retired even if they never had another employment of any kind and were not in fact even looking for employment as a writer.

Ah, you say—Casey Stengel lives! Wrong. That segment—we can't really call it a sentence; the presentation of *a choice* calls for an *either . . . or* resolution, and it never gets to the *or* part—was written by the man who at the time was president of the Writers Guild of America (West), the union to which most screen and television writers belong. If the president of the writers can get off a passage like that, think of the troubles the rest of us must have.

Other points can be considered too. "A word is not a crystal, transparent and unchanged; it is the skin of living thought and may vary greatly in color and content according to the circumstances and the time in which it is used." So Justice Oliver Wendell Holmes wrote, in a 1917 Supreme Court opinion that was well and truly said. There are even occasions when, in the hands of the master, the circumstances and time call for the *wrong* word. Thus Alfred Tennyson at the age of 19 could write:

All day within the dreamy house,
    The doors upon their hinges creak'd
The blue fly sung in the pane; the mouse
Behind the mouldering wainscot shriek'd
    Or from the crevice peer'd about . . .

. . . and a century later, T. S. Eliot would write, *"The blue fly sung in the pane* (the line would be ruined if you substituted *sang* for *sung*) is enough to tell us that something important has happened."

At the same time Eliot was celebrating Tennyson's substitution of *sung* for *sang*, another master, Satchel Paige, was substituting *stang* for *stung*. "I stang him," the baseball immortal declared happily, having plunked a particularly ill-mannered enemy batsman in the sweetbreads with a fastball. Not all of us can hope to misuse the language like a Tennyson or a Paige. But note the misuse they made of it. Had Tennyson correctly written *sang*, it would have sounded flat. Had Paige correctly said *stung*, it would have sounded dull as oatmeal. The operative word in both cases is "sounded." The ears have it.

States Bates and Other Diseases

Because this book is for the everyday citizen, we can isolate some elements of communicating he or she will not often have to deal with—not so often, certainly, as newspapers, magazines, or public relations agencies in their press releases. Taking notice of these elements can be instructive nonetheless. Consider for example the case of States Bates disease, which consists of placing the speaking verb ahead of the speaker (*agrees Smith, swears Hopkins, hopes Davis, promises Ginsburg, croaks Martinelli, states Bates*). Its origin in news and feature stories may be traced most prominently to the early years of *Time* magazine, of which Wolcott Gibbs wrote, "Backward ran sentences until reeled the mind."

Today some publications ban the practice entirely, but most permit it, and the usage can in fact be defended in cases where the speaker is both introduced and identified (*"I am optimistic," said Arthur Hale, chief market analyst for Dow Jones*). Otherwise, natural English prefers that the subject precede the verb, and next time Hale opens his mouth in the story, better *Hale said* than *said Hale*.

Victims of States Bates disease tend to exhibit side effects, and these are more widespread. One of them is the habit of looking for verbs to substitute for *say*, or, having used *say* once, groping indiscriminately to avoid repeating it. At times, particularly when a deliberate effect is intended, a substitute is useful: one of the fine sentences in the language is Ring Lardner's *"Shut up," he explained*. But as a general rule there is nothing wrong with *say/said*, nor any reason to dodge its use more than once in the same piece of writing. Among other things, it keeps the writer safe from such redundancies as *"Oh?" she asked* or *"Oh!" he exclaimed*, where the punctuation has already done the verb's job. (When you get to *"Ah!" he ejaculated*, school is out.)

Preamble

Particularly unfortunate are the fancy ones—*intone, aver, expostulate, declaim,* etc.—and verbs that mistake action for speech (*"Of course," he nodded*—a talking nod?—*"Yes," she smiles; "Maybe," he grinned*). And particularly abused is the verb *state*. *"The bus was early," he stated; The girl states, "It is snowing"; "Don't forget to bring home some ALPO," his wife stated* all are examples of overimportant use of a verb that should be limited to the courtroom or other formal proceedings.

Say is a good old word, and a short one. "Short words are best," Winston Churchill said, "and the old words when short are best of all." Here we might think of Churchill's own *I have nothing to offer but blood, toil, tears, and sweat.* Or some others, like:

> . . . *We here highly resolve that these dead shall not have died in vain; that this nation, under God, shall have a new birth of freedom; and that government of the people, by the people, for the people, shall not perish from the earth.*

> . . . *The energy, the faith, the devotion which we bring to this endeavor will light our country and all who serve it, and the glow from that fire can truly light the world.*

> . . . *Friends, Romans, countrymen, lend me your ears; I come to bury Caesar, not to praise him.*

> . . . *The only thing we have to fear is fear itself.*

> . . . *Surely goodness and mercy shall follow me all the days of my life, and I will dwell in the house of the Lord for ever.*

> . . . *If they're running and they don't look where they're going I have to come out from somewhere and catch them. That's all I'd do all day. I'd just be the catcher in the rye.*

Examples like that make Churchill's point, but they have something else in common: *the absence of adjectives!* Strong writing uses adjectives sparingly and selectively. Some linguists believe that verbs are the strongest words in the language. Others say the nouns. The question is certainly arguable. When a Shakespeare writes:

When beggars die there are no comets seen;
The heavens themselves blaze forth the death of princes . . .

where does the magnificent power in those words come from? Surely not from "magnificent," or any other adjective—there are no adjectives. Most of us grew up learning that descriptive writing is the best kind— and it is. We learned too that the function of adjectives is to describe— and it is. Adding that 2 and 2, we got 5, and the overuse of adjectives has cluttered our ability to communicate ever since.

The adjective has its place (picture the advertiser prohibited from saying "new" or "improved"), and Shakespeare can show us where:

This royal throne of kings, this sceptred isle,
This earth of majesty, this seat of Mars,
This other Eden, demi-paradise,
This fortress built by Nature for herself
Against infection and the hand of war,
This happy breed of men, this little world,
This precious stone set in the silver sea,
Which serves it in the office of a wall,
Or as a moat defensive to a house,
Against the envy of less happier lands,
This blessed plot, this earth, this realm, this England.

Happy (note *less happier* four lines farther on), *royal, little, precious, silver*—these are ordinary words. A lovely exception here or there (*sceptred*), but the strength and beauty in Shakespeare rests in the predominance of basic English (his most famous phrase—*To be or not to be*—is not

Preamble

exactly an overcomplicated piece of wording). Note too the progression of the four nouns in the final line—*plot, earth, realm, England*—from the meanest to the grandest; only the first and weakest needs (and gets) the help of an adjective. All told, in that passage, there are 20 nouns that might have been described by adjectives but weren't.

The reader can readily create his own examples of sentences that use adjectives, then sentences that say the same thing without them. The effect may be surprising. *Masculine* is a good, tough adjective, and surely its use will strengthen a sentence. Or will it? If you had to choose between *He is every inch a masculine fellow* and *He is every inch a man*, which would you choose? No contest. (That example serves an additional purpose in the way it shows how often adjectives—and their kissing kin, the adverbs—serve simply to create redundancy. We assume fellows are masculine; if you mean to say he's a feminine fellow, that's something else. Recently there was a *new innovation* in, of all places, *The New York Times*. And how many times have we seen expressions like *pleasantly cordial* or *savagely vicious*?

Adverbs, like adjectives, are descriptive words, usually describing the when, the where, the how or the how much. While adjectives describe only nouns (as in *descriptive* in the preceding sentence), adverbs can describe other adverbs, adjectives or verbs (as in *usually* in the same sentence). Many adverbs, though not all, become that way just by the addition of *ly* to the adjective (thus the adverb *usually* from the adjective *usual*). In *pleasantly cordial*, the adverb *pleasantly* came from the adjective *pleasant*. So *controversial* becomes *controversially*, *hopeful* becomes *hopefully*, and *hopefully* becomes, in the words of Edward D. Johnson, author of *The Washington Square Press Handbook of Good English*, "perhaps the most controversial usage in the language."

The very extent of the literature on *hopefully* can knock your hat off. In his book *On Language*, William Safire wrote: "Six years ago, in my first appearance as a newspaper columnist, I vowed never to offend readers with any of the words then rampantly in vogue: *relevant, meaningful, knowledgeable, hopefully, viable, input, exacerbate, dichotomy*, and the ambivalent use of verbs as *program, implement*, and *structure*.

"Since then I have adopted *hopefully*, because no other word better substitutes for the awkward 'it is to be hoped that.' . . . 'Hopefully' had a reason for being: There is no 'hopably' or 'hopedly,' and the alternative—'one hopes' or 'it is to be hoped'—is hifalutin. The word has few defenders (my 'shame on you' file is bulging after the defense in this space) but it surely has a multitude of users."

Dick Cavett, writing in the pages of *Vanity Fair*, remembered a sign outside the porch door of author Jean Stafford: "Anyone misusing the word 'hopefully' on these premises will be prosecuted." James Atlas, writing in *The Atlantic Monthly*, remembered the same sign differently: "Use of the word 'hopefully' not permitted on these premises." Geoffrey Nunberg, a teacher of theoretical linguistics at Stanford University who supervised the writing of the usage notes for the second edition of *The American Heritage Dictionary*, has written, "Most of the members of the *Harper Dictionary of Contemporary Usage* panel who condemn [*hopefully*] give no reason at all: Shana Alexander calls it 'slack-jawed, common, sleazy'; Phyllis McGinley says it is an abomination, whose adherents should be lynched; Harold Taylor says it makes him physically ill; and so on. Now, I do not doubt the sincerity of these passions, but I wonder what arouses them."

Whatever it is, it arouses passions abroad as well. Here is a letter published in *The Times Literary Supplement* of London:

Sir,—Perhaps we have not quite caught up with the Germans as I said in my letter of February 27 (and I must add the Dutch, with *hopelijk*), because alongside *hoffentlich* they also have *hoffnungsvoll* (*hoopvol*) and so the ambiguity against which Charles Monteith recently warns us does not arise for them. Clarity must certainly be the criterion in any linguistic question. Hence, if we really want such an adverb (and the Romance languages manage quite well without one), we must either adopt some neologism such as "hopedly" (three syllables) on the analogy of "reportedly" (cf. in today's paper [March 13]: "She was reportedly presented to King Gustav"), or we must make the rule that "hopefully" in the new sense is only good English when it is the first word in the sentence.

34 Watersmeet, Northampton

First word in the sentence or not, *hopefully* is still in trouble. *Hopefully, the Red Sox will make four errors in the first inning.* Strictly speaking, the only thing in that sentence that *hopefully* modifies is the Red Sox—and surely the Red Sox don't hope to start off with four errors.

What's happened is that *hopefully* here has been changed to mean, as another letter to *The Times Literary Supplement* suggested, simply *God willing.* It is the speaker, not necessarily the subject of the sentence, that is doing the hoping. Often the person doing the hoping, in strict construction, isn't a person to begin with. In his book, *A Treasury for Word Lovers*, Morton S. Freeman gives as examples "Hopefully, the program will end soon" and "Hopefully, the ship will anchor near the shore." As Freeman points out, "These examples say that the program and the ship are full of hope—a meaning, of course, not intended."

But take it for its *God willing* connotation and, as Geoffrey Nunberg asks, what's wrong with it? Answer: nothing. Nothing, except for one small ingredient, and that is that scratch a person who uses "hopefully" once in a conversation and you'll find a person who uses it 46 times. It's a crutch word. When speech material is prepared at Manning, Selvage & Lee, we try never to use *hopefully*, and for that very crutch-word reason. It's like eating peanuts: you can't eat only one.

And all of this arose from what? From adding *ly* to an adjective to form an adverb, that's what. Thankfully, it doesn't happen all the time (and *thankfully* is in the same boat as *hopefully*—so are *sadly* and *sorrowfully* and *happily* and *mercifully* and *frankly* and *truthfully*, and frankly and truthfully, we seldom recommend using *frankly* or *truthfully* even when they are grammatically correct.

16

A new situation comes into play here. It isn't an element you're likely to see discussed by Safire or Nunberg or Freeman or *The Times Literary Supplement*, because no grammatical rules, let alone passions, are involved.

Nevertheless it goes directly to the gut of good communicating. Whoever starts you off with "Frankly," or "Truthfully," or "Candidly," or "To be perfectly honest," is not only setting you up but killing his own message. One of the most common mistakes in communication— again, it has nothing to do with the rules of grammar—is the announcement that you're being truthful and above-board. The only thing this conveys is that up till now you've been something other than that. Announcing that you are not a deceptive person makes you out, almost automatically, to be a deceptive person. Otherwise, why the announcement?

One good test of communicating lies in the reaction to it . . . not in the way the message is phrased but the way it's received. Think back to your favorite movie, and the scene where bad news came over the telephone. How often do you see the news being announced? Almost never. What you see instead is the person receiving the news. You never describe the moon, Chekhov said; what you describe is the reflection of the moon in a broken piece of glass in the bed of a stream.

Hopefully, then, no sentence we say or write will ever begin with *truthfully*, whether we are violating the rules of grammar or not. And equally hopefully, let us make it a rule to review what we intend to say or write and try to go easy on the *-ly* endings, and all other unnecessary suffixes as well. Bill Zinsser calls *hopefully* an "atrocity." What then shall we say about the *-ize* endings ("We are going to prioritize our findings") or *-wise* ("New Year's Day will be a great day for football on TV collegiatewise") or *-able*? A favorite here is *analyzable*, meaning capable of being analyzed. Give that a little thought before you put it to any use. Analyzable is a debutante at some Deep South cotillion: "Analyzable, you come here this instant! I do declare!"

Tucker's Law

Of course it is useful to know the rules, and a good number of years ago, the late Ernest Tucker, then assistant city editor of the old Chicago *American*, set down his own memorable list of twelve. We reproduce it here as Tucker's Law:

1. Don't use no double negatives.

2. Make each pronoun agree with their antecedents.

3. Join clauses good, like a conjunction should.

4. About them sentence fragments.

5. When dangling, watch your participles.

6. Verbs has got to agree with their antecedents.

7. Just between you and I, case is important.

8. Don't use commas, that aren't necessary.

9. Try to not ever split infinitives.

10. It is important to use your apostrophe's correctly.

11. Proofread your writing to see if you any words out.

12. Correct speling is essential.

The last two—number 11 and number 12—speak for theselves and will no elaboration here. But it can be fun, and a gainful thing, to take up the others.

1. *Don't use no double negatives.*
Actually the use of the double negative has its place. The rule is that two negatives make a positive, three negatives make a negative, and four negatives make somebody like Frank Howard, who became manager of the New York Mets and spoke of player trades: "It's nothing that I don't think you don't really feel or realize isn't going to happen."

But with infrequent, judicious use, there are times when the double negative says something a little different, and a little more correct than the single positive. You use some original math on your income tax return. You figure your chances of getting audited are maybe 1 out of 20. The audit notice comes, and sure enough it challenges that one piece of math. If the odds were 1 out of 20, you can't say the audit was *expected* (single positive). Given the funny arithmetic, you can say it *wasn't unexpected* (double negative).

The double negative also serves the cause of wry or mordant understatement. If only 60 percent of a city's fleet of buses are operating, would you say the service was *operative* (single positive)? More accurately, you'd say it *wasn't inoperative* (double negative), meaning the service was running but you could hardly tell. If 96 percent of the teachers at a school are women, *almost totally female* would be the single-positive way of saying it. *Not totally male* uses irony to say the same thing and may make a point all its own.

The most commonly encountered double negatives are followed by *but*: *I wouldn't say he was dishonest, but . . . She may not be unhappy, but . . . The survey may not be inaccurate, but . . .*

But watch out for *but*. Like *however* and *nevertheless*, it carries a negative connotation. It's a way of flipping the coin to its opposite face, an expression of "on the other hand," and to reflip it in the same sentence, or even the neighborhood of the same sentence, can be disconcerting. Example, from a New York newspaper:

> Lebanese and Israeli spokesmen said the confrontation began when the Israeli vehicles tried to pass through the checkpoint, but they gave conflicting accounts of what ensued, but both sides agreed that no shots were fired.

The *but . . . but* sequence is troublesome. How much better it would have read as:

> Lebanese and Israeli spokesmen said the confrontation began when the Israeli vehicles tried to pass through the checkpoint.

The two sides gave conflicting accounts of what ensued, but both agreed that no shots were fired.

Some additional editing there, but the main purpose was to get it from two *but*s down to one. We can say that *but* shouldn't be used twice in the same sentence; we can say too that it shouldn't be the first word in two consecutive sentences: *It was raining. But the weatherman said it would clear up. But it didn't.* Take out the second *but*. Make the final sentence: *It didn't.* See how much stronger it just became.

We're coming in stages here to *however*, another form of *but* and home of one of the most common grammatical mistakes found in the language today. When used in the sense of *but*, *however* is a weaker word, and it needs punctuation—not after but before. Let us again enlist the Red Sox: *We got three runs in the top half of the first inning, but the Red Sox came back with four in their half.* Nothing wrong with that. But put it this way . . . *We got three runs in the top half of the first inning, however, the Red Sox came back with four in their half* . . . and you've got a new ball game. The *however* dangles, enclosed by commas, and could as well refer to the way our side got its runs (*however = in whatever way*) as it does to what in this case it really means: "*but* the Red Sox came back."

As mentioned, this is a very common mistake. It's all right to enclose *however* in commas if it's not the first word in its statement. *Smith said, however, that he felt better* is fine. *However, Smith said that he felt better* is also fine. What isn't fine is *Smith said that he felt better, however, Jones felt worse.* So the formula is this: Whenever *however* is used to mean *but*, and is the first word in its statement, it should start a new sentence.

2. *Make each pronoun agree with their antecedents.*
It's all out for the sack race here. What are pronouns? They're *I, you, he, she, it, we, they,* and in various forms *me, him, her, us, them, who, whom, which, this, that, whose, mine, yours, its, their, theirs, our, ours, all, any, one, anyone, anybody, no one, nobody, most, none, some, whichever, whoever, whatever, ourselves, myself, yourself, itself,*

yourselves, themselves, every, everyone, everybody, and some others, and when your wife knocks on the door and you say, "Who's there?" and she says, "It's me," she's using incorrect English, because correct English insists on "It's I." Which nobody in her or his right mind would say.

Worse than that, we're jumping ahead to Tucker's rule number 7. Let's backtrack to the last sentence of the foregoing paragraph: . . . *nobody in her or his right mind* . . . and look at the way the pronouns agree with their antecedent. The phrase *her or his* is a straight cop-out, forced on us by the feminist movement. Today we can no longer begin a business letter with the salutation *Gentlemen:* or *Dear Sirs:* (try *Dear Persons:*—it takes a little getting used to, but it may be the new way).

Meanwhile, nobody in his right mind wants to go around saying "Nobody in his or her right mind," but that's the point we've reached, and the temptation to say the hell with it and go "Nobody in their right mind" becomes stronger all the time. *Nobody* is singular and *their* is plural, so *nobody in their right mind* is just plain wrong, and nobody in their right mind believes otherwise (*believes* is singular, agreeing with *nobody,* but *their* is still plural, so we've just made the situation worse).

The feminist movement isn't all that new, really. H. W. Fowler, whose classic work *Modern English Usage* was first published in 1926, was talking about it even then. He set up the following choices:

A.   . . . *as anybody can see for himself or herself*

B.   . . . *as anybody can see for themselves*

C.   . . . *as anybody can see for himself*

"No one who can help it chooses A," Fowler wrote. "It is correct, and is sometimes necessary, but it is so clumsy as to be ridiculous except when explicitness is urgent.

"B is the popular solution; it sets the literary man's teeth on edge, and he exerts himself to give the same meaning in some entirely different way if he is not prepared, as he usually is, to risk C.

"C is here recommended. It involves the convention that where the matter of sex is not conspicuous or important, *he* and *his* shall be allowed to represent a person instead of a man. Whether that is an arrogant demand on the part of male England, everyone must decide for himself (or for himself or herself, or for themselves)."

Half a century later, John Simon would write:

> The fact that some people are too thickheaded to grasp, for example, that "anyone" is singular, as the "one" in it plainly denotes, does not oblige those who know better to tolerate "anyone can do as they please." The correct form is, of course, "anyone may do as he pleases," but in America, in informal usage, "can" has pretty much replaced "may" in this sense, and there is nothing more to be done about it; but we cannot and must not let "one" become plural. That way madness lies. And don't let fanatical feminists convince you that it must be "as he or she pleases," which is clumsy and usually serves no other purpose than that of placating the kind of extremist who does not deserve to be placated. The impersonal "he" covers both sexes.

In his article "The Decline of Grammar" in the December 1983 issue of *The Atlantic Monthly*, Geoffrey Nunberg quotes both Fowler and Simon, then says:

> . . . I stick with *he* as an impersonal pronoun, except where sex neutrality is important. I think there are good syntactic reasons for my choice, though I know syntacticians who would disagree with me. But grammar can only excuse my usage, not justify it, and all its arguments are irrelevant for people who have decided to go with the use of *they* on the grounds that *he* is sexist. As Fowler maintained, matters of conscience must take precedence.
>
> This takes me to . . . the question of courage and tolerance.

When I ask myself why I have decided to stick with the use of the singular *he* to refer to an antecedent like *every American*, I find that my motives are unclear.

Intuition tells me that the singular makes grammatical sense. But I am troubled that English grammar requires the singular to be of one gender or another, and that precedent requires it to be masculine. And I have sometimes supposed that it is only out of fear of being thought ignorant that I don't move to using *they* and *them* in all cases.

It may be that *they/them/their* will become more and more accepted. For an all-male gathering, it would be right to say, "Everybody in the room cast his vote," and for an all-female, ". . . *her* vote," but either of those singulars would be wrong if the gathering was a mixture of both sexes, and to say, "Everybody in the room cast *his or her* vote," might sound as though each person voted more than once. Besides, *his or her* could be a plural expression, and so might take not *vote* but *votes*!

The easiest way is surely: "Everybody in the room cast their vote." It is grammatically wrong, but the fact is that usage does not follow rules. Rules follow usage.

Collective nouns—where the same word can be either singular or plural—present fewer problems, and sometimes we can see singular and plural standing side by side, as in "Montgomery Ward *says they'll* deliver the mattress tomorrow." *Says*/singular, *they*/plural, and so what? Among purists, the majority says it's wrong, but equally correct is that the majority *say* it's wrong, so the majority have (has) their (its) own problems. The one thing we musn't do here is keep switching back and forth. Having established which degree of number we want to carry the thought, whether singular or plural, we had best stick with it the rest of the way. *The majority say it have its own problems* is not English as she is properly spoke or wrote.

So far in this section we've been talking about *singular* (one) versus *plural* (more than one). In the past, there was the additional question of *two* versus *more than two*. Two of the most common examples here were *each other* (versus *one another*) and *between* (versus *among*), and the traditional rule here was that you used *each other* and *between* for two, *one another* and *among* for more than two. Great writers and speakers throughout history have violated that rule so often that today's dictionaries have pretty much given up on the issue, and indeed there are cases where clarity demands such violation, as in saying, "The trains run between New York, Philadelphia, Baltimore and Washington." To say the trains run *among* those four cities makes it sound as if they don't run so much as they mingle.

There are still some cases, though, where the old rule should be observed. "Given a choice among New York, Philadelphia, Baltimore and Washington, where would you most like to live?" More than two cities there, and *among* is the proper word. Get it down to just two, and you wouldn't say ". . . among New York and Philadelphia." There, you'd use *between*.

But *each other* and *one another* have become virtually interchangeable. It's totally possible for a husband and wife to love each other one minute and hate one another the next. In his album notes for a recording of the three boogie woogie pianists Albert Ammons, Meade Lux Lewis and Pete Johnson, George Lines wrote, "They had a curious ability to play together without hindering each other's style and yet support one another to a degree that must have been unique among pianists."

Note the correct use of *among*, but note also that *each other* and *one another* are both used to describe the same three people. Nor was this just a careless piece of writing: the *each* in *each other's style* plays up the singular individuality of each; the *one another* in *support one another* underscores something held in common. Mr. Lines found a way both to violate and observe the old rule at one and the same time!

And note now, if you will, the word *both* in the preceding sentence. *Both* of course means two, and it is well to remember that its placement in a sentence can be important. Of the following two sentences, which is correct?—

A. He is friendly both with his ex-wives and their new husbands.
B. He is friendly with both his ex-wives and their new husbands.

Answer: Either is correct, unless he has more than two ex-wives, in which case A is right and B is wrong. That's if you're writing it. If you're speaking it, both are correct! Try sentence B out loud for yourself, and assume you're talking to someone who doesn't know the man's marital history. If the man has more than two ex-wives, your voice will automatically dip down when it says *both*, then give extra emphasis to *ex-wives*, and that will tell your listener there were more than two. If on the other hand the man had only two wives, your voice just as automatically will give more stress to *both*, less to *ex-wives*.

Finally, in this discussion of number and singular versus plural, comes one of the most popular mistakes in English usage: the matter of people who say *less* when they mean *fewer*, and vice versa. Actually, the amount of vice versa is minimal. People do use *less* when they mean *fewer*; as for *fewer*, some people don't use it at all.

Many books on grammar have long, complex dissertations on the difference between those two words, but this is one case where a truly simple formula comes into play: Use *less* to describe the singular, *fewer* to describe the plural. And a simple way to remember that is to think of the advertising slogan, "Fewer calories, less fat." Calories (plural) = *fewer*, fat (singular) = *less*. No chance of getting the slogan mixed up, because it can't be said the other way around. "Less calories, *fewer fat*"??

Plural here means just that—more than one. The age of a person may be 50, but that's one number, not more than one, and we're applying it to just one person. Thus we would say, "He's less [not fewer] than 50." Or, "This is the first day in the last two weeks that the temperature's been less than 90." But: "The game attracted fewer than 10,000 spectators," or, with *spectators* left unsaid, still, "The game attracted fewer than 10,000."

The word *under* can be used too, but as a synonym for *less*, not *fewer*. This gives us three words on the "minus" side—*fewer, less, under*; and that makes things interesting, because there are only two equivalent words on the "plus" side—*more* and *over*. *More* is the equivalent, then, of both *less*, which takes the singular, and *fewer*, which takes the plural; and what are we supposed to do about that?

The solution is to let *more* take the plural in all cases, and *over* take the singular. Thus, "He's over 50," and "This is the tenth straight day of temperatures over 90," but "The game attracted more than 10,000 spectators."

3. *Join clauses good, like a conjunction should.*
And Winston tastes good, like a cigarette should (to quote another familiar ad slogan). It should be, as a professorial follow-up commercial pointed out, *as*, not *like*. Why? Because *as* is a conjunction, like *or*, *and*, or *but*, and so what follows it will have a verb. *Like*, on the other hand, is a preposition, so all it takes is a word or phrase. If the slogan had just said, "Winston tastes like a cigarette," *like* would have been correct.

All right, then, what about "He treats his employees like dirt"? *Dirt* is a single word and there is no verb, so *like* is the correct word, right? Wrong. What we are saying there is, in effect, "He treats his employees the same way dirt treats them," and of course that's not what's meant. What's meant is, "He treats his employees as though they were dirt."

That brings us to a useful guideline, set down by Frank O. Colby and cited by Roy H. Copperud in *Webster's Dictionary of Usage and Style*: "If *as*, *as if*, *as though* make sense in a sentence, *like* is incorrect. If they do not make sense, *like* is the right word."

This one's most likely a losing battle. More and more, *like* is coming to be used as a conjunction, like the song lyric, "*I'm gonna love you like nobody's loved you, Come rain or come shine.*" But we also get things like: "Like her mother, the kitchen was her favorite place." Her mother looked like a kitchen?

4. *About them sentence fragments.*
Speaking in incomplete sentences is something all of us do.

> "Going someplace?"
> "The beach."
> "Don't you wish."

"Wrong with the beach?"
"With what?"
"Dollar eighty-five."

The dialogue can go on forever, perfectly comprehensible to both parties. In written form, the incomplete sentence is routine for announcements ("No smoking," "Closed Mondays"), directions ("First left after traffic light"), headlines in many newspapers (SHOOT MOM FOR 50 CENTS), correspondence ("Great weekend. Loved party. Maureen over her cold?"), and the inevitable "Wish you were here."

All this is unremarkable stuff. The sentence fragment, used deliberately for effect, has its place. See it at work here in William Styron's *Sophie's Choice*:

> She died a disgusting death, in a transport of pain. Amid the heat of July, seven months later, she faded away in a stupor of morphine, while all the night before, I pondered over and over those feeble embers in the cold smoky room and speculated with dread on the notion that my abandonment that day had sent her into the long decline from which she never recovered. Guilt. Hateful guilt. Guilt, corrosive as brine.

The last three sentences—*Guilt. Hateful guilt. Guilt, corrosive as brine*—aren't sentences. They're fragments—masterfully crafted, with a build to them as powerful as *This blessed plot, this earth, this realm, this England*. The meter of the two differs totally. Shakespeare's lines are a succession of perfect iambic pentameter. Styron has a sentence 58 words long, suddenly followed by a single word: *Guilt*. In our mind's ear we hear the beat of a muffled funeral drum:

DUM   (roll)   DUM   (silence)   DUM   (roll)   DUM
GUILT hateful GUILT   (silence)   *GUILT corrosive as BRINE*

It is not expected of us, nor likely, that we march to the dactyls of Styron's drummer. In fact, the fewer fragments we try, the more impact

Preamble

they'll have. A good drill is to use complete sentences and nothing else. The more we do this in what we write, the more we'll find ourselves *talking* in complete sentences as well. Listen to Ted Koppel or Gene Shalit on television: they speak in complete sentences, not fragments. Or listen to Vin Scully broadcasting a baseball game. The transcribed tape recording of his description of the final half-inning of Sandy Koufax's perfect game against the Chicago Cubs on September 9, 1965, reads as though it had been scripted in advance.

5. *When dangling, watch your participles.*
Walking across the street, a bus hit the man. Subject of that sentence is *a bus*. The bus wasn't walking, the man was walking.

It's usual to see participles defined as the *-ing* form of a verb, but actually they can come in all shapes and sizes, and with equally unnerving results. *Bought for $750,000 in 1979, Mr. Nixon sold the apartment for $1.8 million*. The participle there is *bought*. (The sentence itself is from a newspaper story.) Was Mr. Nixon bought for $750,000?

And there are groups of words, variously participial (and appositive, and prepositional, and adverbial) phrases, that can dangle the same way: *A man for all seasons, his home was in London*. His home may be many things, but a man it's not. As Edward D. Johnson has said, "Many dangling constructions aren't as famous as the dangling participle but are just as common."

And even when they avoid the dangle, participles and their relatives can cause grief. Incorrect is *Crossing the river, the afternoon was spent by them in New Jersey*. The afternoon didn't cross the river. So we eliminate the dangle and make it, *Crossing the river, they spent the afternoon in New Jersey*. Here's news: It's still wrong. Why? Because the two actions, crossing the river and spending the afternoon, come across as taking place at the same time, where obviously New Jersey came second. *Doing my homework, I took the test and passed it* involves three actions: doing the homework, taking the test, and passing it, and they happened in that order. So in effect we have a dangle there too, this one not of subject but of time. I did my homework before the test, not during it. *Looking out the window, the taxicab was waiting* means the taxicab looked out the window. *Looking out the window, we* (or whoever) *saw the taxicab waiting* is in all ways right: *Looking* agrees with the subject *we,* and the looking and seeing took place at the same time.

The foregoing examples have in common that they don't really sacrifice clarity. So what if A *man for all seasons, his home was in London* has a dangling appositive phrase? Its meaning is totally clear, and there is nothing wrong with the sound of it. *Looking out the window, a taxicab was waiting* is lousy English, and educated people will even laugh at it and hold it up as an example of what's gone wrong with our society, but the meaning remains clear enough.

The real problem is that those who dangle indiscriminately will inevitably create at least some sentences that are at best ambiguous. *George met Fred going to the bank* does not tell us who was going to the bank—George, Fred, or both. Some teachers say the automatic way to avoid this is simply to eliminate the participle and recast the sentence without it. But that doesn't always work. *George met Fred on his way to the bank* still doesn't tell us who was en route to the bank; indeed, *on his way to* simply replicates *going to.* The solution there is instead to recognize the participle for what it is—an adjective—and put it so that it modifies its subject. If it was George headed for the bank, then *Going to the bank, George met Fred.* If it was Fred, then *Going to the bank, Fred met George.* (Now we *can* substitute *on his way to* for *going to* and the meaning still comes clear: it wasn't the change of words that was needed; it was changing their position in the sentence.)

Again the thing to remember is that participles and related unattached phrases are essentially adjectives. In *Running because he was afraid, a heart attack struck the fat, elderly man* we make it seem that a frightened, running heart attack (and a masculine one at that!) struck an elderly fat man. In that sentence, there are four adjectives describing the man: *running, afraid, fat, elderly.* The problem was one of position: the first two came before *heart attack,* the last two before *man.*

If we redo it as: *Running because he was afraid, the fat, elderly man was struck by a heart attack*, all four adjectives now come before *man*, the word they're there to describe, and we've eliminated the dangling participle. The trick lies in recognizing that *running* is here an adjective, no different from *afraid*, *fat*, or *elderly*. What if we'd substituted *aging* for *elderly*? What's the difference between *aging* and *running*? There is none. Both are adjectives made from verbs.

One reason good writers don't dangle participles is that they know better. Another is that they don't use that many participles to begin with. Participles are adjectives. Adjectives are weak words.

6.   *Verbs has got to agree with their subjects.*
We covered this under point number 2 of Tucker's Law—at least in its application to number: singular versus plural, two versus more than two. There remains another kind of agreement, this one in terms of *time*.

Suppose you had a conversation with Mr. Smith yesterday about an election taking place tomorrow. You're describing that conversation today:

A.   I talked with Smith, and he said Jones would win.

B.   I talked with Smith, and he said Jones will win.

C.   I talked with Smith, and he says Jones will win.

Question: Which of those is correct? Answer: Nowadays, all three. (But that will be so only until the votes are counted tomorrow night. From that point on, only A can be used. We can't apply the word *will*, as in B or C, to something that's already happened. Nor can we apply the word *says*, as in C.)

There was a time when only version A would have been accepted— this is a throwback to the strict sequence of tenses in Latin grammar— and there remain some grammarians who will not accept such an innocent-sounding sentence as "I would have liked to have been there." (It was okay, though, to say either "I would like to have been there" or "I would have liked to be there.") But these and similar rules are being relaxed. *Will* is moving in to take over all the territory once reserved for *shall*; and more slowly, *was* is taking over for *were*: before long, the *were* in "If I were king" will become a *was*.

The present tense can be used to follow the past tense to state a present-day fact: *Columbus said the earth* is *round*. (But *Queen Isabella said it* was *flat*.)

Finally, in the case of the composer Richard Wagner, who always said he does his best work in a cold climate, we must of course substitute *did* for *does*, because he is no longer composing. He is decomposing.

7. *Just between you and I, case is important.*

Tucker is right (and *Tucker is right* is right, even though Tucker, like Wagner above, is no longer with us; the *is* is acceptable for Tucker because what he said describes an existing truth). Case *is* important, and it's remarkable how many otherwise civilized people go around saying "Between you and I," and "It's important to he and I," and so forth. "*Is it he whom I was going to see* or . . . *him whom* . . . ?" Geoffrey Nunberg has written. "Only the ear knows." Another tribute to the part *sound* plays in the language.

Prepositions—*between, to, for, into, in,* our old friend *like, with, without, of, except, during, from, through, under, over, about, across, on, after, around, before, above, out,* and so forth—usually consist of one word; they can also consist of several: *in addition to, on account of, in spite of, as well as, in regard to, out of,* etc. They take the objective case, which in most instances is a fact without significance, since the objective case of almost all nouns is the same as the subjective.

Thus, a house that stands in the woods is a subjective *house*—*house* is the subject of the verb *stands*. If we paint that house, it's now objective—the subject now is *we*, and the house is the object that got painted. But it's still *house*. And if we use a preposition and go *into* the house, once again it's objective—the object that was gone into—but once again, still *house*.

So we can draw up a table:

Preamble

Subjective	Objective
house	house
cat	cat
boat	boat

But:

I	me
we	us
he	him
she	her

And we can not go around singing, "For I and my gal." The bells are ringing for *me* and my gal, because we have used the preposition *for*, and that takes the objective pronoun *me*, not the subjective *I*. That's the rule; besides, the ear doesn't like *for I*.

An additional word about prepositions: One old rule insists we can never end a sentence with a preposition. No one knows what that rule's all about. Or whose mouth it came out of. (No law against consecutive prepositions either. A story in the March 12, 1984, issue of *Sports Illustrated* refers to a drug investigation that had "zeroed in on up to" ten members of the same team.)

In matters of case, meanwhile, we must confront *who* and *whom*. "There are word-lovers who live to catch out the mighty in a misused *whom*," Nunberg has written, and indeed, what with *whoever* and *whomever*, not to mention the grandiloquent *whosoever* and *whomsoever*, we are surrounded by the temptations of sin. *Who, whoever, whosoever* all are subjects; *whom, whomever, whomsoever* all are objects. So we can extend our table to read:

Subjective	Objective
who	whom
whoever	whomever
whosoever	whomsoever

. . . and if you're trying to settle a dispute, you try to learn who hit whom first. But wait, you say: in that sentence, isn't *who* the object of the verb *learn*? And if so, shouldn't it be that you try to learn *whom* hit whom? The answer is that the object of *learn* is the entire clause *who hit whom*, not just the first pronoun, and *who* is the proper subject of that clause.

If it comes to a choice of villains here, *whom* is the winner. "The most loathsome word (to me at least) in the English language is *whom*," Kyle Chrichton, the veteran editor, wrote. "You can always tell a half-educated buffoon by the care he takes in working the word in. When he starts it I know I am faced with a pompous illiterate who is not going to have me long as company." And George Ade wrote, " 'Whom are you?' said Cirro, for he had been to night school."

You make a phone call and an unfamiliar voice answers. Do you say, "Whom am I talking to?" or "Who am I talking to?" Strangely, if we were to "diagram" those two sentences, we could "prove" that both were right. The first one would come out:

I	am talking	to	Whom
(subject)	(verb)	(preposition)	(object)

. . . thus justifying the objective *Whom*. And the second would go:

(It is)	Who	(that)	I	am talking	to
(implicit predicate)	(main subject)	(implicit pronoun— object of *to*)	(secondary subject)	(verb)	(preposition)

. . . thus justifying the subjective *Who*.

In real life, we do no diagramming, and it is a caution the way role models, such as newscasters, will mistake *whom* for *who*. "The tickets are available to whomever wants them"—evidently the speaker believed that since *whomever* followed *to*, a preposition that takes the objective case, then the objective *whomever* had to be. Again here, the true object

Preamble

(in this case, the object of *to*) is not the single pronoun but the entire clause, and correct grammar for the clause is *whoever wants them*. Or a famous sportscaster: "I asked him, 'Whom do you think are the ones to watch out for.' " . . . "On deck is Darrell Porter, whom as Keith articulated held this team together." Or these examples, from Fowler's *Modern English Usage*:

> *Speculation is still rife as to* whom will *captain the English side to Australia.* . . . *There is quite a keen rivalry between father and son as to* whom is *to secure the greater share of distinction as a cattle breeder.* . . . *There has been some speculation as to* whom *the fifth representative from South Africa was.* . . . *The French-Canadian, who had learned* whom *the visitors were, tried to apologize to Prince Albert.*

"The mistake is a bad one," Fowler wrote, "but fortunately so elementary that it is nearly confined to sports reporters." He may have been half right: elementary, *sí*; confined to sports reporters, no.

In a great number of instances, the choice is so obvious (*Who lives in that house? . . . to whom it may concern*) that no problem arises. But when there is doubt, a good, if somewhat novel, working rule is to go with *who* instead of *whom*. It may not be right every time, but the degree of error will be smaller—and therefore less noticeable.

8. *Don't use commas, that aren't necessary.*
This brings us face to face not just with the comma but with the dreaded *thatwhich*. When do we use *that* instead of *which* and vice versa? Great literature can be found using both, as with Shakespeare's *robs me of that which not enriches him*, or *That which comes after ever conforms to that which has gone before*, from the *Meditations* of Marcus Aurelius; but great literature is not of any help to us in this particular inquiry. We have a different construction in focus, exemplified in the following two sentences:

A.   The fence, which is made of cedar, gives excellent protection.

B.   The fence that is made of cedar gives excellent protection.

Which of those two is correct? Depending on the intended meaning, either one. In the first case, the meaning is that the fence gives excellent protection—and incidentally, it's made of cedar. In the second, the meaning is that any cedar fence gives excellent protection. In the parlance of grammarians, *that* is "restrictive"—it defines; *which* is "nonrestrictive"—it just adds further information.

Now let's read the two sentences aloud. See what happens to the voice as we read. In example A, where the cedar part is additional information, we have a natural pause after "fence," and another pause after "cedar." But in example B, where cedar defines the kind of fence that gives excellent protection, we say the sentence straight through, with no pauses. We indicated the pauses in A with commas; no pauses in B, so no commas.

In front of us, then, is a quick, reliable way to know when to use *which*, and when to use *that*. If the voice pauses, use the comma and *which*; if no pause, no comma and *that*.

Most people use *which* when they mean *that* more often than the other way around. Strunk and White, Niswender, and others recommend a "which-hunt": having written something, go over it, find those *which*es that are used to define instead of amplify, and make them *that*s instead.

9.   *Try to not ever split infinitives.*
Compound parts of verbs—*has gone, might want, will strike*—like to stay together, but there is no almighty rule about it. So, *has recently gone, might at times want*, or even greater separation—*will for the most part strike*—display nothing more than unremarkable everyday usage. And there's really no structural difference between splitting compounds like those and splitting infinitives, except for the frequency with which the split infinitive tends to regrettably irritate the ear and to by and large jangle the nerves. You might say you plan to stay home from work

tomorrow. You'd never say to home stay or to home from work stay. And Hamlet didn't say "To be or to not be."

So split infinitives are good things to avoid. Try them aloud and see whether the adverb or adverbial phrase in between the *to* and its verb might not sound better someplace else. Most times it will. Not always. Which sounds better—*I didn't want to actually come right out and say it,* or *I didn't want to come right out and actually say it*? Either way, the *actually* splits an infinitive, the first time *to come*, the second *to say*, yet either is a logical, unforced and agreeable-sounding way to give it that little extra nudge of emphasis.

Some purists, to be sure, are sworn never to split an infinitive. Problem there is that sometimes there's no other choice. In *I told him to clearly translate written queries from the Syrian, Bulgarian and Nigerian delegations, as well as the British,* where the hell else in the sentence can the *clearly* go?

William Safire quotes George Bernard Shaw on this subject: " 'Every good literary craftsman splits his infinitives when the sense demands it.' He called for the immediate dismissal of the pedant hired to chase split infinitives and concluded: 'It is of no consequence whether he decides to go quickly or to quickly go.' " Let alone *decide quickly to go*, where in trying to avoid the split infinitive we actually can change the meaning, with *quickly* describing not the way he will go but the way he decides.

10. *It is important to use your apostrophe's correctly.*
The old-time Hearst columnist Arthur "Bugs" Baer once did a retrospective piece about a baseball game whose box score listed somebody named L'n'h's'r in center field for the Detroit Tigers. "Today nobody knows whether his name was Loopenhouser or Lagenhassinger," Baer wrote, "and I bet his wife still calls him a liar when he says he once played on the Detroits."

The apostrophe is used, as in L'n'h's'r, to indicate missing letters (or numbers—this passage is being written in '84). It's used also in contractions (*o'clock, isn't, won't, we'll, he's, wasn't,* etc.), and to show possession (*the car's engine, the housewife's dilemma, all the king's men*), and to indicate some plurals (there are five *s*'s in "possesses"). Once in a while the same word uses two apostrophes, one for contraction, the other for possession (*Mrs. O'Leary's cow*). And once in a while we find possessives strung together consecutively. (For good communicating, *my sister's roommate's lover's friend's bedroom's window opens onto the courtyard* also opens onto four possessives too many.)

As for the final *s* following the apostrophe in the possessive case, we note an exception: possessive pronouns (with or without an *s* in their base form—*yours, mine, his, her, hers, yours, ours, their, theirs*) never take an apostrophe.

There's a pronoun missing from that list: *its*. Like the others, its possessive form doesn't take an apostrophe. If you're a boss, try to tell that to your secretary. Even worse, if you're a secretary, try to tell it to your boss. People who'd never dream of depicting *a subject of her's* or *a house of their's* will give you *a color of it's*. *It's* is a contraction, short for *it is*. It's not a possessive. Its possessive is *its*.

This is a matter of punctuation, not spelling. We've already said this book would not take up spelling. Either way, the case of *its/it's* would supercede that intention. People who wouldn't even notice the misspelling of *supersede* in the previous sentence will stamp you for an illiterate if you misuse *its*. So better don't.

Throw the Baby out of the Window a Penny

> It was unlikely Reagan would cancel the grain deal, an act opposed by the U.S. farming community.

What does the farming community oppose? The grain deal or its cancellation?

Another one, from the same newspaper:

Preamble

> Gov. Cuomo was angrily attacked by feminists last year when he signed the anti-nudity bill because it made no exceptions for breast-feeding.

Was the governor attacked because the bill made no exceptions, or did he sign it because it made no exceptions? The Cuomo sentence doesn't tell us. What it does give us is another illustration of the most common mistake made in communicating—the sloppy ordering, or punctuating, of the thoughts we're trying to express.

In the Cuomo example, the simple insertion of a comma after *bill* would have brought clear the intended meaning, if that meaning was that he was attacked for signing a bill that made no exceptions. If the meaning was that he signed the bill *because* it made no exceptions, put the comma after *year* instead, and once again the thing becomes clear.

But surely there are times when a simple comma is not going to save the situation. Generations of lawyers have beseeched us to show them our letters before we mail them, with an eye to what Frances Ferguson, in her essay *The Unfamiliarity of Familiar Letters*, has called "the extraordinary difficulty of being interpreted as one intended." But lawyers themselves have stood similarly accused. In the anthology *The State of the Language*, edited by Leonard Michaels and Christopher Ricks, a piece by David Levine says, "As for the myth that lawyers speak with grace and power, one need only examine the verbatim transcript of an oral exchange among lawyers and judge, or an examination of a witness, to know how inarticulate most lawyers seem when forced to utter intelligible sentences without benefit of a second draft."

But what of lawyers when they put their thoughts in writing? The title of Levine's article is: "My Client Has Discussed Your Proposal to Fill the Drainage Ditch with His Partners." Levine got the title from an actual lawyer's letter cited in an article by Richard C. Wydick in the *California Law Review*.

The problem as Levine sees it lies "in placing the modifying words too far from the word being modified." That's a good way of putting it, and it's wrong to say that lawyers are any more guilty than the rest of us. Take for example the following television listing in *The New York*

Times: "Powerful drama of mistreatment of American Indians by the old master, John Ford." *The New Yorker* reprinted that one, with a comment of its own: "The dirty rat."

The *Times* entry is a perfect example of Levine's definition of the problem. The modifying words do indeed occur too far from the word being modified, which is *drama*. Before getting to the old master, John Ford, we get to mistreatment first. So the drama by Ford becomes instead the mistreatment by Ford.

How would we fix it? There are several ways. One of the quickest and easiest—and one which requires no additional words (a factor when space is at issue)—would be just to substitute one two-letter word for another: "Mistreatment of American Indians in powerful drama by the old master, John Ford." The line may not win the Nobel Prize for literature, but at least *The New Yorker* will have no cause to reprint it.

The problem here is universal, the plague of professionals and non-professionals alike. Hardly an edition of your daily newspaper can be found that does not contain at least one confusing arrangement of words. And, to quote Strunk and White, "How swiftly meaning departs when words are wrongly juxtaposed." The authors give several examples— "You can call your mother in London and tell her all about George's taking you out to dinner for just sixty cents" is just one of them, leaving the reader to "wonder which cost sixty cents—the phone call or the dinner."

You'd fix that one by making it, "For just sixty cents you can call your mother in London and tell her all about George's taking you out to dinner." But sooner or later we must depart from listing specific examples and proposing a remedy in each case. There are too many of them. "The writer must bring together the words and groups of words that are related in thought and keep apart those that are not so related." So says the Strunk and White book *The Elements of Style*. But this is far easier said than done.

The drill we suggest goes back to the beginning pages here: Use your ears. Take whatever you have written, regardless of whether you intended it to be spoken or read, and have it read aloud. Ideally, that reading will be done by somebody else, seeing the copy for the first time. If that isn't workable, do it yourself—but pretend you're somebody else. Read it slowly, saying to yourself "This is all brand new to me." If it's ambiguous, the ear is more likely than not to catch it.

The next step is to set things right. If no ready way occurs to you, it may be that you tried to cram too much into the offending sentence. Solution: Turn it into two sentences. Another Strunk and White example:

> Major R. E. Joyce will give a lecture on Tuesday evening in Bailey Hall, to which the public is invited on "My Experiences in Mesopotamia" at eight P.M.

One way to change that would be to make it:

> On Tuesday evening at eight, Major R. E. Joyce will give a lecture in Bailey Hall, to which the public is invited, on his experiences in Mesopotamia.

But we might still be trying to get too much information into a single sentence. Strunk and White recommend something better:

> On Tuesday evening at eight, Major R. E. Joyce will give a lecture in Bailey Hall on his experiences in Mesopotamia. The public is invited.

And note, incidentally, that turning it into two sentences required fewer words overall than either of the one-sentence examples. Certainly that saving in words will not result in every case, nor is it any particular goal. Most times it will be an outright impossibility. But when we consider the alternative—trying to pack everything into the same sentence—we risk getting results like this one, from a newspaper account:

> The Yankees were trying to break a spell of two successive losses in which they dropped two games of three in Minnesota

and lost to Texas Thursday night after arriving back home at 4:30 that morning.

Mixed Metaphors, Overkill, and The Evil I

A second barrier to good communicating is one that most people, offhandedly at least, would seldom suspect. The overall term for it is "mixed metaphor." Here are just three examples:

> *We don't want to jump out of the frying pan if it serves as a good umbrella.*
> *It's a place where the hand of man has never set foot.*
> *There's no point in milking a dead horse.*

We can remember hearing, years ago, a campaign speech by a man running for some local office in the town of Ardsley, New York. "That's water under the dam," he said. Alerted by a snicker from the audience, he was quick to correct himself. "I mean, water over the bridge."

In the conviction that colorful language is the key to effective communication, many people will reach for the nearest-remembered figure of speech. At best, if they remember it correctly, it will be a cliché. And to avoid that, they reach for another and combine them.

Now they have something new and original. And it comes out like the examples listed above.

Why do we view this as so serious a flaw in communication? Because its effect is the last thing a communicator wants: people laughing when they're not supposed to. The sports reporter who depicted Olympic swimming champion Mark Spitz "churning through the water like a house afire," or his colleague who hailed a new baseball season with the "The dawn of a new era comes at 8:15 tonight," were committed to vivid description—and getting their laughs in the wrong places.

Preamble

A third cardinal sin in communicating is overkill. The word itself came into general use no more than fifteen years ago, when it began to be used to describe stockpiling of nuclear weapons, but it's a good one, and its home in the language is secure. It's used now to depict overstatement and exaggeration, and it can be ruinous to the salesperson peddling goods or services, although not all of them seem discouraged by that risk.

But the curse of overkill is not confined solely to the world of sales. It pervades all areas of writing and conversation. To overstate is to place your listener or reader "instantly on guard," as E. B. White puts it— "everything that has preceded your overstatement as well as everything that follows it will be suspect in his mind because he has lost confidence in your judgement or your poise. . . . A single overstatement, wherever or however it occurs, diminishes the whole, and a single carefree superlative has the power to destroy, for the reader, the object of the writer's enthusiasm."

Putting it another way, next time you're introduced as "the funniest person in the world," you'd better be funny.

One other enemy of effective communication will be mentioned here, and that is the vertical pronoun. The word *I* is used too much. So many occasions require it that no real argument can be mounted against it. It's still used too much. Sometimes it *should* be used, but the speaker or writer goes out of his way to avoid it—perhaps to affect a false modesty, perhaps to give added weight to his own opinion by implying it is shared by others. It's still used too much.

Jones asks Smith how long it takes him to commute to work. Smith tells him. Jones then tells how long it takes *him* to commute. This may not interest Smith. Yet the urge is universal not only to inject oneself into a conversation, but to steer the conversation to that end.

It may be, in fact, that Jones was so busy planning his own account of his own commute that he hardly heard Smith's answer. Devising what it is you are about to say about yourself is the fastest and surest way to lose concentration on what somebody else is saying.

Perhaps you can quote yourself verbatim from your last phone call. Can you quote the other party verbatim? Or let's say you're asked to write an essay of at least 250 words on your thoughts about the most personal, self-centered act of all—suicide. Could you do it without once using *I*? (Hamlet managed it—see again "To be or not to be. . . .")

Actually, then, there are two points at work here—curtailing references to ourselves, and listening to others. "The art of diplomacy," one United Nations ambassador said, "is to think twice before you don't say anything." That's part of the art of communicating, too.

Part 2

GLOSSARY

The Right and Wrong Stuff

English is a crossbred
Worldian language.
It is interwoven with Anglo-Saxon,
Old German, Sanskrit, Latin and Greek roots,
Interspersed with Polynesian, Magyar, Tatar, et al.
The largest proportion of English words
Are derived from India's Sanskrit,
Which itself embraces hundreds
Of lesser known root languages.

Those are the words of the legendary R. Buckminster Fuller in *Synergetics*, his view of the geometry of thinking. "Unfortunately," Dana Niswender writes, "English is not the world's most consistent language." He was speaking from the standpoint of spelling, but as we have already seen, he could have included almost everything about the language . . . except for its richness and power. English has taken, and continues to take, more from all other languages than any other tongue in history, and today, most of all, it is taking from itself.

One result of this, paradoxical in the midst of the recession in literacy in the United States, has been the emergence of a golden age in American writing. Mourn lost heroes and vanished times though we may, it is doubtful that any period in letters has produced contemporaneous novelists so gifted as Saul Bellow, William Kennedy, Philip Roth and William Styron. And one reason for this, feckless though it can at first appear, may be that they have more words to work with.

Some of these words are new. But just as many, if not more, are old words being put to additional uses. It comes as something of a shock to realize that barely a generation ago, few people if any were *chairing* a meeting, *hosting* an event, *featuring* an attraction, *positioning* something, or, God forbid, *contacting* anybody. Even as these words are written, another battalion of nouns, like *gift* and *impact*, is invading the turf of the verb. "It may be," Geoffrey Nunberg has written, "that

Glossary

my children will use *gift* and *impact* as verbs without the slightest compunction (just as I use *contact*, wondering that anyone ever bothered to object to it)."

The fact is that many authorities do object to it, even today, and in the case of the newer invaders, like *gift* and *impact*, Nunberg is among them: "I can't overcome the feeling that it is wrong for me to use them in that way and that people of my generation who say 'We decided to gift them with a desk set' are in some sense guilty of a moral lapse, whether because they are ignorant or because they are weak. In the face of that conviction, it really doesn't matter to me whether *to gift* will eventually prevail, carried on the historical tide. Our glory, Silone said, lies in not having to submit to history."

The remainder of this book, consisting of a glossary of words, phrases and terms, must be inevitably prejudicial therefore. We do not accept, for example, that the noun *loan* can be used as a verb when *lend* is already there for that purpose, even though the banking community not only accepts it but is its most frequent user (or abuser). By the same token, we do not agree that *utilize* should never be used (we're told we should use *use* instead). We do agree that *utilize* should seldom be used, but seldom and never are not the same, and every now and again, when a special *utility* of the object is the thing in point, then *utilize* is the word that will better bring out that point. *He used his house key as a can opener* can have the implication that house keys generally can be used as can openers. *He utilized his house key as a can opener* better describes the unusual nature of the act, and the ingenuity behind it. And one other thing: *He used his house key as a can opener* doesn't necessarily mean he succeeded in opening the can. *Utilized* carries the stronger connotation of success.

With that preamble, on to the glossary. The entries appear in alphabetical order; so do several of the dilemmas. So anyone interested in the difference between *infectious* and *contagious* will find it under *c*, as **contagious, infectious.**

abbreviation, acronym Some people refer to initialized expressions like IOU or FTC as acronyms. They're not—they're abbreviations, because you say the letters aloud one at a time. An acronym is its own word, made from the initials of other words, so that NATO rhymes with Plato. Like Plato, *acronym* is ancient Greek, but for all that heritage it is one of the most recent words in our language. Webster's Second International and *The Oxford Universal Dictionary*, both revised through the mid-20th Century, don't even list it! The Evanses, in *A Dictionary of Contemporary American Usage*, say that the acronym "seems largely an outgrowth of World War II, though WRENS [from Women's Royal Navy Service] was coined in World War I." They also say, "There seems to be no generally applicable agreement as to which abbreviations become acronyms and which do not." Some, like IRS, are unpronounceable, so the letters have to be sounded one at a time, but it is one of life's little mysteries why NATO became an acronym but OPA, pronounced not "opa" but "O-P-A" with all initials sounded, didn't. As for HUD, some people say it as an abbreviation, pronouncing all three letters— "H-U-D"—while others say it as an acronym—"hud." Go figure.

ability—see *contagious*

accident, episode, event, incident An *accident* is an accident. An *episode* is one of a series of happenings (separate from, but arising out of, the main subject). An *event* is a major happening. An *incident* is a minor happening, and one of brief duration, occurring in the course of an episode or event. *Incident* is also the word defense lawyers use to describe an accident.

advise, inform Advice is opinion or counsel; information is news. *Advise* is to be avoided when *inform* is meant. Sometimes both are to be avoided. *This is to inform you that the queen is away* is better than *This is to advise you that the queen is away*. What's best, most likely, is *The queen is away*.

affect, effect   To *affect* something is to have some influence on it; to *effect* it is to make it happen. The difference in meaning is known to almost everyone, and almost everyone uses the words correctly in conversation. (At least, we assume they are using them correctly. Since they sound the same when spoken, nobody really knows.) So strictly speaking this entry doesn't belong in this book; it's a reminder in spelling.

Used as a noun, *effect* means outcome or result. The use of *affect* as a noun is affected by the fact that there is no such noun, except in a narrow use in psychology, to mean a feeling or an emotion.

after—see *following*

aggravate, irritate   To *aggravate* is to take something that *irritates* and make it worse. Thus we *aggravate* a skin *irritation* by scratching it.

ain't   Here's a table of contractions:

you're not	aren't you	you aren't
he's not	isn't he	he isn't
she's not	isn't she	she isn't
it's not	isn't it	it isn't
we're not	aren't we	we aren't
they're not	aren't they	they aren't
I'm not	aren't I	I _____

Only thing interesting here is the blank. Just one of the renegade aspects of English is that while it's perfectly acceptable to say "aren't I," it's totally unacceptable to say, "I aren't"!

Aren't I glad I can't say "I aren't"? Maybe I'm not glad. The larger point is that the word *ain't* entered our lives not just as a vulgarism but also because somebody left a hole in the language.

Those holes are there. We might say that this person or that building exceeded the height limit by 2 inches or 22 feet, or was short of the height limit by the same margin, but why do we use three words—*was short of*—to express the opposite of the single word *exceed*? The reason is simple: used in that context, there *is* no single word to express the opposite of *exceed*!

Getting back to *ain't*: No literate person will use this word, which is as good a reason as any to use it every once in a while. Its occasional use varies the rhythm and texture in speech and writing, and shows the user to be conversant with all forms of the language, not just the right ones. But not too often, pray.

almost—see *nearly*

alternate, alternative   These words aren't interchangeable. *Alternative* involves a choice (some people even say "alternative choice," which is tautological, like calling a mountain Summit Peak), while *alternate* simply means "the other one." At least, that's what it used to mean. Today, it can mean "another" as well as "the other." The words have in common that, like *between* and *each other*, they once were reserved for expressions of two. But usage has relaxed that restriction, and concepts of more than two, as in *You have several alternatives*, or *The team has a regular goaltender and three alternates*, are accepted by all but the most severe pedants. (*Alternate*, as an adjective, always did have a separate application to mean every other one in a series, as in *The code uses alternate letters of the alphabet*. As a verb, *alternate* can be used even more loosely: *She alternated with several others as our receptionist* is okay.

A.M./P.M.   *I called you at 9:40 A.M. this morning* is wrong. A.M. already means morning, just as P.M. means any time between noon and midnight. In the example here, *today* could be substituted for *this morning*, or—even better, because it's more naturally conversational—eliminate the A.M. and make it *9:40 this morning*.

amateur   The word comes from the Latin verb "to love." One of the greatest golfers in history, Bobby Jones, played for the love of the sport and never got paid for it, which made him an amateur (rather than the professional who gets paid). He was also a better golfer, in his heyday, than any who did get paid.

Today we apply the opposite meaning, holding the amateur to be a blundering bungler. It probably is too late to alter this latter-day definition. Robert Littell, the novelist, has defined the professional as "someone who thinks that if something is worth doing, it is worth doing well." An amateur, Littell says, "is someone who thinks that if something is worth doing, it is worth doing badly."

amaze, astonish, surprise   Time was when *amazed* meant one thing (literally, lost in a maze—bewildered), and *astonished* another (literally, turned to stone). Today they are used interchangeably. To be *surprised*, however, means simply to be taken unawares. A favorite story among grammarians has it that the wife of Dr. Samuel Johnson, the lexicographer, discovered him kissing the maid and exclaimed, "I am surprised!" "No," he said, "*I* am surprised, *you* are astonished."

Why the maid let him kiss her is another question, since he bathed only infrequently. "You smell," the maid said to him. "No," he said, "*you* smell. I stink." He was a slovenly, morbid, myopic, melancholic, absent-minded man who in 1755 published a dictionary of the English language that stood for nearly a century as the finest work of its kind ever produced. His ability not only to grasp but to define the distinctions between words has never been equaled, even though time and usage may have eroded the distinctions themselves. Today, alas, everybody uses *smell* the way the maid used it.

Anyway, *amaze* and *astonish* (and for that matter *astound*) can nowadays be used pretty much interchangeably, but they are not the same as *surprise* (or for that matter *startle*).

and/or   *We can give you a national and/or regional program*. We've all seen that *and/or* expression in writing. But how many times do we use it when *talking*? Basic rule: If you don't say it, don't write it. *We can give you a national program, a regional program, or both* says what is meant. To Strunk and White, in *The Elements of Style*, *and/or* is "a device, a shortcut, that often leads to confusion or ambiguity." Beyond that, it just doesn't sound right. That's why we so seldom say it out loud.

as far as x is concerned   This is a good, workable phrase that has been systematically shortened, often by television newscasters who should know better, to just *as far as* and now pervades both the spoken and written language in that way. The entire phrase should be used. You'd say, "As far as I'm concerned, Harry is an idiot." If you said instead, "As far as I, Harry is an idiot," then Harry is not alone. To say, "As far as Pittsburgh is concerned, the air quality is better than it was," is to say Pittsburgh's air has improved. To say, "As far as Pittsburgh, the air quality is better than it was," means the air is better only till you reach Pittsburgh. Similarly, "As far as the parking lot is concerned, it's safe," means a safe parking lot; but "as far as the parking lot, it's safe," means watch out when you get there. So truncating the phrase is not only displeasing; it can be confusing as well.

as, so   Some teachers insist that *so* should be used when the sense is negative (*not so deep as a well*, instead of *not as deep*), but most people use *as* either way, for the negative as well as the positive, and Roy Copperud, in his *Webster's Dictionary of Usage and Style*, writes, "The idea that *so* is required with *not* has no grammatical basis." Copperud is comforting in another use of *as* too, giving the example of a sentence that requires four *as*'s to be grammatically correct—"He likes to be known as a philosopher as much as as a theologian"—and terming it "half-*as*'d." This isn't a problem that comes up very often. More frequently, we have to deal with pairs like *as . . . than*—*This year's weather is as bad or worse than last year's*—which, to be correct, should read *as bad as or worse than*. Very few people think to supply the extra *as*, and very few people notice the omission.

assume, presume   We can *assume* anything, true or false, sight unseen. Unfortunately, we can and do *presume* the same way, although presumably *presume* should have some weight of evidence, statute, or logic in its favor. The law still *presumes*, rather than *assumes*, that a citizen is innocent until proved guilty, but erosion is setting in. An example given by Morton Freeman in 1983, showing proper use of *presume*, was "Since they are living together, I *presume* they're married." Uh-oh.

assure, ensure, insure   Each means something different. To *assure* is to impart confidence or certainty; to *ensure* is to make certain; to *insure* is to indemnify or safeguard. The Evanses have a nice example: "To be well insured ensures peace of mind and is vastly assuring."

average, mean, median   Nine people work in the same office. One of them earns $14,000 a year; three others earn $16,000 each; the five others earn, respectively, $18,000, $20,000, $22,000, $38,000 and $65,000.

The *average* salary for that office is $25,000—a figure reached by taking the total payroll of $225,000 and dividing it by the number of employees. The *mean* salary is $39,500—the figure halfway between the lowest salary ($14,000) and the highest ($65,000). The *median* salary is $18,000—exactly the same number of people earn less than $18,000 as earn more than $18,000.

Noteworthy: The average salary may be $25,000, but nobody earns exactly that amount, and only two of the nine people in the office earn more. And nobody earns exactly the mean salary of $39,500, and only one person earns more!

Typically, we are wont to say "average" when what we really mean is **typical** . . . or *common, ordinary, prevailing*. But in the example given here, the only correct word to describe the figure $25,000 is *average*—yet even though it is used correctly, it gives a false picture of the office salary structure. We not only say it wrong, we hear it wrong! The *median* salary of $18,000 is far more *typical* for that office than either the average or the mean.

Once we depart from the world of numbers, *average* takes on even less meaning. We say "the average Canadian," even though there is no such thing. What we mean is the *typical* Canadian.

A batting average in baseball is exactly that—an average. The average temperature for the month of July is exactly that—an average. But such instances where *average* is used correctly are in the minority, and it's not a bad idea to restrict its use, substituting some other word (like *typical*) in all non-numerical situations, or in numerical cases, like the salary example given above, where the true average is simply misleading.

The average reader will pay no attention to this suggestion.

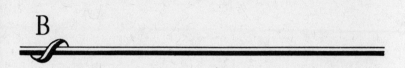

B

begin, commence, start   All three mean the same, and *begin* is the best of them. *Start* is okay for machinery, like clocks and locomotives, and certainly for horse races. *Commence* should be reserved for formal occasions, and even then, if it weren't in the dictionary it wouldn't be missed.

behalf   Great sections of printed space are taken up by the grammarians' books on when and whether it should be *in behalf of* as opposed to *on behalf of*. The unabridged edition of *The Random House Dictionary of the English Language* says that if you mean to say "as a representative of or a proxy for," you should use "*in* or *on* behalf of," while if you mean to say "in the interest or aid of," you should use "*in* or *on* one's behalf." *The Shorter Oxford English Dictionary* says to use *on* when you mean "on the part of, on the side of," but *in* when you mean "in the name of, in the interest of." The *Funk & Wagnalls Standard Dictionary* says *behalf* means "the interest or defense (of anyone): preceded by *in, on* or *upon*." A salute to Funk & Wagnalls for not caring one way or another, but even there, with its reference to "anyone," F&W is limiting *behalf* by saying it can be used only when applied to people. Actually, it can be used for things or abstractions just as well. If you want to make a speech in (or on) behalf of eggplant, go ahead.

belabor   *Don't belabor the point* is a syllable too long. What's correct is *Don't labor the point*, meaning don't keep pressing it. To *belabor* is to physically attack (split infinitive and all).

beside, besides   *Besides* means "also," "in addition to." *Beside* means "next to," as in *I left it beside the lamp on the table beside my bed*. Besides, *beside* can be one of those words, like *sanction*, *overlook*, and *suspicious*, that means the opposite of itself—not only "next to" but also "away from"—but that might be beside the point.

bi-   This means either two or twice, so if we say "bimonthly" do we mean 6 times a year or 24? Convention has settled this to mean every two months; if we mean twice a month, we substitute *semimonthly*, *semi* meaning half. Same rule for weeks and years. America's bicentennial in 1976 came after 200 years, not 50.

   Those who don't trust the convention can play it safe. A line in Manning, Selvage & Lee's bimonthly newsletter says, "Published six times a year."

bilateral, multilateral, unilateral   In order, these mean having two sides, having many sides, having one side. So behaving *unilaterally* means acting on your own; a *bilateral* agreement is one reached by two parties; and *multilateral* goes for three or more. But while these words could apply to almost anything, their most customary application is to political behavior.

broad, wide   According to Fowler, "*Wide* refers to the distance that separates the limits, and *broad* to the amplitude of what connects them." Bergen Evans calls that a "brilliant analysis." What the mayor of Philadelphia may call it is something else. There's a Broad Street there, and in many other places, and a Broad Avenue in Leonia, New Jersey, and many other places. But how many communities have a Wide Street?

   Harry Shaw, in his *Dictionary of Problem Words & Expressions*, says, "*Broad* is preferable when the word it modifies is a surface or expanse viewed as such (*broad* stream, *broad* field, *broad* shoulders). *Wide* is preferably used when the sense of space is stressed (the table is four feet *wide*) or when the distance across a surface is mentioned indefinitely (The lake is *wide* at that point)." The mayor of Philadelphia may have a problem with that too, but Shaw puts us on the track of something, with his table that's four feet *wide*.

There's an implication, in the use of *wide*, of side-to-side measurement. *Broad* can refer not only to width but to length (the broad jump at a track meet is known also as the "long jump"). *Broad* has a more mature ring to it: granted that either word could go either place, we are more likely to refer to a broad grin on the face of an adult, a wide grin on the face of a child. *Broad* deals with the general, the figurative, the conceptual; *wide* with the specific, the literal, the measurable. *Broad*, then, has a meaning grander than *wide*. That is why there are so many Broad Streets instead of Wide Streets. (The next street over from Broad Avenue in Leonia is Grand Avenue.)

burglar, robber   The *robber* accosts you in person, using either violence or the threat of violence. The *burglar* gains entry to your house in the expectation that nobody's home. If you're sitting in your car and somebody points a gun at you and takes your wallet, he's a robber. If he opens the car when you're not there and takes your wallet off the seat, he's a burglar. (If he takes the whole car, he's a *thief*.)

C

capacity—see *contagious*

center around/on   *My thoughts are centering around the report we discussed yesterday* is wrong. A center is a single point. We should use *on*, not *around*.

cheap, inexpensive These words should be used to describe goods, services, or their purveyors (*an inexpensive dentist*), rather than the price being charged; the word to describe such a price is *low*. As for the difference between *cheap* and *inexpensive*, the former has a shoddy connotation— *He does it on the cheap . . . That was a cheap trick to play. Inexpensive* is more diplomatic, although, like *budget-minded* or *thrifty*, often also a euphemism. An excellent word here is **reasonable**.

childish, childlike *Childish* is an expression of scorn or criticism, in description of an adult's behavior. *Childlike* is used for the good traits, like *childlike* wonder, *childlike* trust. **Infantile** is even more scornful than *childish*.

classic, classical They mean the same thing—something of the highest class, the optimum grade of workmanship or performance, the ultimate—but *classical* is reserved for the time of ancient Greece and Rome. *Classic* is used—and, sadly, overused—for anything else, from a classic golf swing to a classic head cold. What's called for is a classic case of restraint.

collaborate together Since *collaborate* already means to work together, to *collaborate together* means to work together together.

college, university A *college* awards undergraduate degrees, a *university* graduate degrees, and a university comprises two or more colleges. It's an engaging paradox that while those things are true, making the *university* the more embracing entity, *college* is given the more embracing meaning in the language. Thus, *He's going to college to become an architect*, or *a survey of college-educated women*, both use *college* to include *university*.

colon Should what follows a colon start with a capital letter? Answer: not if it's not a complete sentence. But what if it *is* a complete sentence? A *Dictionary of Contemporary American Usage* says, "Either a capital letter or a lower-case letter may be used after a colon. If a full sentence follows the colon, it generally starts with a capital."

Generally, but not always. *As he ran past, I noticed only one thing about his clothing: his shirt was blue* is better than . . . *His shirt was blue,* because the color of his shirt is subordinate to the major thought that there was only one thing I noticed about his clothing, and therefore doesn't justify the larger importance of the capital letter. If, on the other hand, *As he ran past, I noticed only one thing about his clothing: He wasn't wearing any,* we just shifted the major thought, and the capital is right.

commence—see *begin*

comparative, superlative degrees This is a minefield. We say "new, newer, newest," and "heavy, heavier, heaviest," but "generous, more generous, most generous," and "constant, more constant, most constant." What dictates the *-er* ending for some adjectives in the comparative degree but the use of *more* for others? Or, for that matter, the *most* for the superlative degree in some cases, the *-est* in others?

To feel our way through this one, we can start with adjectives that end in *y*. They take *-er* and *-est*, as with the example of *heavy* above, or *lovely, lovelier, loveliest,* or *silly, sillier, silliest.* We're talking adjectives, remember, not adverbs. The adjective *happy* becomes *happier, happiest.* But the adverb *happily* becomes *more happily, most happily.* (Exception: Frank Loesser's "Most Happy Fella.")

Adjectives of one syllable also take the *-er* and *-est* forms: *Bright, brighter, brightest; rich, richer, richest; close, closer, closest;* unless they are words that aren't often used in comparisons—words like *just, real, right.*

The ear plays a principal role in all of this. To single out a clever fellow, we might say, *"He is the cleverest of the three."* Less happily: *"He is the cleverer of the two,"* for in *cleverer* we have piggybacked one *er* sound on top of another. Thus: *clever, more clever, cleverest.*

There are irregular forms—*good, better, best; bad, worse, worst . . .* superlatives—*foremost; hindmost; utmost . . .* dialect forms—*only, onlier, onliest* . . . and doubled forms—Shakespeare's *"That was the most unkindest cut of all."*

There are even times when we can go both ways, as in, "Of the three *most stupid* things I ever read, this is the *stupidest.*" And there are a number of adjectives that shouldn't take comparative or superlative degrees at all. Since a circle is *round* to begin with, there can be no such thing as a *rounder* or *roundest* circle. The same principle can be applied to adjectives like *square, level, equal, faultless, entire,* and *unanimous.* Some grammarians include in this list *conclusive, outstanding, perfect,* and *whole,* but the most outstanding way of making this point more conclusive might be to say you can find legitimate exceptions in the cases of words like those. Some can really fake you out. *Certain* would seem to be an adjective that shouldn't be compared, but there is nothing wrong with making more certain or most certain that this is so.

The most famous adjective in this no-no group is **unique** (see its entry later in this glossary). This one not only doesn't take *more* or *most*—it doesn't take anything.

compare to/with In comparison between persons, concepts or things of the same classification, *with* is used; if they are dissimilar, then *to.* Most concert pianists believe that compared *with* a Yamaha piano, a Steinway piano makes a better sound. Compared *to* a Yamaha motorcycle, a Steinway piano also makes a better sound.

complement, compliment Like *affect* and *effect,* these words are hard to misuse in conversation, because they sound the same; thus no one can tell whether you understand the difference between them. To *compliment* is of course to praise; to *complement* is to fill out or complete. The noun forms are spelled the same, and mean the same, as the verbs.

comprise A tricky word, neatly analyzed by Morton Freeman: "Although a whole comprises parts, parts compose a whole. . . . 'Twenty-five players comprise the full complement of a professional baseball team' should be stated the other way around. It is the full complement that comprises twenty-five players."

Best advice as to how to use *comprise* might come down to one word: Don't. The word adds neither elegance nor erudition to anyone's vocabulary and any urge or need to use it can be banished by the use of *composed of* (or *consists of*) instead.

concept, idea, notion   These three are arranged here in alphabetical order, but they happen to go progressively from the most to the least careful. A *concept* is an idea that has been worked out, in fairly extensive, if not complete, form. A *notion* is just a passing idea, usually spur-of-the-moment. An *idea* is halfway between *concept* and *notion*. And a fourth word—**conception**—connotes a finished *concept*.

All that having been said, the fact remains that the distinctions among these words are extremely fine.

consensus   A *general consensus of opinion* is a classic (see **classic**) redundancy: it starts at the middle and works both ways. In and of itself, *consensus* means general agreement, so *general* is unnecessary; it also already means collective opinion, so *opinion* is equally unnecessary. If this were a book on spelling, it would also point out that many people misspell it *concensus*, doubtless because it has the sense of *census*. Freeman calls this one "possibly the most commonly misspelled word in the English language, excepting 'supercede' for *supersede*."

consistently, constantly   *Consistently* is constantly misused to mean *constantly*. It doesn't. *Consistently* means unchanging; *constantly* means all the time. To say, "She consistently changes her opinions" is to say she's inconsistent. (If she constantly changes her opinions, she's also inconsistent.)

constant—see **continual**

contagious, infectious   A *contagious* disease is one that's transmitted by touch—body, clothing, drinking glass, whatever. An *infectious* disease travels on its own, as through the air. (Either one can make you **nauseated**, but not **nauseous**. If you're nauseous, you make other people nauseated. Good illustration here of the difference between **ability** and **capacity**—one may have the ability to be nauseous, the capacity to be nauseated.)

contemporary, contemporaneous Both words describe people or things existing at the same time, but *contemporary* also means the present. If that can cause confusion in a given context, use *contemporaneous* instead.

contentious, controversial Controversy exists in the view of others, contention in the manner of self. A man who is both (a) *controversial* and (b) *contentious* is (a) subject to controversy and (b) capable of stirring it up.

continual, continuous Something that happens frequently and with regularity is *continual*; if it happens all the time, without interruption, it's *continuous*. *The bus service is continual* means the buses run one after another. *The bus service is continuous* means one long bus. **Constant** is a synonym for *continual*; **incessant** is a synonym for *continuous*. All of these words are continually being misused. In fact, they are **perpetually** misused. Nobody seems to mind.

contrast As a verb, *contrast* takes *with*: *He contrasted the 1984 Yankees with the 1927 team.* As a prepositional phrase (*in contrast*), it takes *to*: *In contrast to the 1927 Yankees, the 1984 team was a joke.* As a noun, *contrast* can take either *with* or *to*: *If you want to make a contrast of the 1984 Yankees (with/to) the 1927 team, lots of luck.*

controversial—see **contentious**

convince, persuade Different shades of meaning here. *Persuading* is done more through appealing or advising, *convincing* more through presentation of evidence or proof. Rightly or wrongly, *persuade* also smacks more of the underhanded. Few lawyers will say, "The jury was *persuaded* that my client was innocent." They'd rather say the jury was *convinced*.

copy, replica All that has to be said about a *copy* is that a copy is a copy. A *replica* is also a copy, but strictly speaking the only time that word should be used is when the copying is done by the maker of the original.

corespondent, correspondent   These aren't variations of the same word. A *correspondent* is one who sends information in writing. A *corespondent* is the other man, or the other woman, in a divorce proceeding brought on grounds of adultery. It used to be *co-respondent*, but see the subsequent entry here under **hyphen**. You may also wish to see a lawyer.

credibility, credulity   *Credibility* is believability; *credulity* is readiness to believe. A curious note is that the same people who have all kinds of trouble differentiating between those two words have no problem at all distinguishing between their negatives, *incredible* and *incredulous*. Someone listening to an *incredible* story may well be *incredulous*.

But one more curious note: Does a newspaper story of a man who drank 48 consecutive glasses of beer put a strain on *credibility* or *credulity*? The answer is either or both.

One other word enters here: **creditability**. This has to do not with believability but with something or someone deserving of praise, honor, esteem. In financial circles, *creditability* (adjectival form: *creditable*) deals with one's entitlement to bank credit.

credit   Credit should be reserved for good performances, not bad, but is frequently misused by sportscasters ("He was accredited with a poor throwing arm") and others.

criteria, criterion   There's no such thing as *a criteria*. If we mean one of the *criteria* we must say "a criterion," or "one criterion," or even "the only [or sole] criterion." Similarly, we can not say "two [or more] criterion." Plural number takes *criteria*.

Exception: The phrase *more than one* takes the singular: *The sponsors had more than one criterion for success.* But this is true of many words: *There was more than one person in the room. . . . Will we see more than one tiger in the cage?* The number *one* requires the singular state.

D

dash   The uses of the dash—and there are several of them, are not really at issue here. Most people use it correctly, and, save for a tendency on the part of some to overdo it, the use ranges from effective to harmless. Its greatest misuse is in punctuation. In the first sentence of this entry, the clause introduced by a dash—*and there are several of them,* ought to have been followed not by a comma but by another dash. Used to set apart a passage in mid-sentence—such as this one—the dash must appear aft as well as fore.

The foregoing sentence is, incidentally, a good illustration of overdoing the dash. The phrase *such as this one* is too unimportant to merit dashes. Nice, unobtrusive commas would have done fine.

data   Is it singular or plural? Time was it was plural and only plural (the singular was, and still is, *datum*). But nobody uses *datum* any more, so *data* can be used either way. But not both ways, please. At least not in the same sentence.

democracy, republic   If the people govern directly it's a *democracy*; if they govern through elected representatives it's a *republic*. As anyone who lives in California, with all its "initiatives" and "propositions" on the ballot, can attest, the United States is both a democracy *and* a republic: first we elect legislators to represent us, then we turn around and legislate directly at the polls.

deny, refute   To *deny* is simply to say it isn't so. To *refute* is to *prove* it isn't so.

deprecate, depreciate   The words look, sound, and mean almost the same. A certain deprecatory remark, for example, can also be depreciatory. The difference is this: *deprecate* means to disapprove;

depreciate is to devalue or belittle. So to *depreciate* your contribution to a winning cause is not necessarily to *deprecate* it.

design, intend Common usage now freely substitutes *design* for *intend*. In and of itself, *intend* means intentional. *Design* doesn't have to. If your house is so *designed* that you get the western sun in your bedroom, that doesn't mean you *intended* it to be that way. Next time you use *design*, stop to think whether it wasn't *intend* (or **plan**) that you meant instead. *The protective bottlecap is designed to be childproof* is correct. *The protective cap is designed to be on sale in stores within a month* is incorrect: *intended*, or *planned*, would be used. There is nothing about the design of the bottlecap that has to do with how soon it will be distributed.

desperate, hopeless *Desperate* may not be quite as bad as *hopeless*. Nothing is more hopeless than *hopeless*.

dictionary game Take four or more people, equip them with pencils and identical slips of paper, and have one of them open a dictionary and read out a word that nobody in the room recognizes (there are thousands of such words in any decent dictionary).

Now everybody invents a definition for the word—everybody except the person with the dictionary, who writes down the actual definition, or a close paraphrase of it. Having done that, the dictionary reader collects all the other definitions, shuffles them into any random order, and reads them aloud, one by one, including his own.

Now, at a signal, everybody, excluding the dictionary reader, votes for the definition he thinks is the likeliest one.

The player who copied the real definition from the dictionary gets one point for every player who failed to guess it.

Any other player gets three points for correctly identifying the true definition, and two points for each vote his own definition got from anyone else.

The object of the game, therefore, is to guess the right definition while at the same time tricking as many others as possible into guessing yours.

Once the points have been totaled, the dictionary passes to another player and another round commences. A game ends when each player has had a turn with the dictionary.

In a typical round, there may at times be one or two similar-sounding definitions; more often there is a wild, sometimes hilarious disparity. Once in a while the weirdest or funniest definition will turn out to be the real one. We recollect *swanimote* as one of the words in a game. Out of a whole variety of definitions, the silliest was "A meeting in a forest." But that's what *swanimote* means.

die from/of After death, or at least after *die*, may come an adjective (*He died poor*), or an adverb (*She died slowly*). In citing the cause of death, *of* is almost always preferable to *from*: *He died of cancer. She died of pneumonia. He died of fright. She died of a broken heart.* An interesting exception would be: *He died from overwork.* What is there about *overwork* that brings this on? It starts with *o*, that's what. Following *of*, it becomes a clumsy locution—*of overwork*—for which *from overwork* is the ready remedy. Cf. everybody's favorite school song: "We are the girls from Overbrook High!"

different from/than Here's a classic example of the correct usage being overtaken by the incorrect. Almost every time we say "different than" we mean "different from," but it is too late to do anything about it.

differentiate, distinguish To *differentiate* is to find differences in detail; to *distinguish*, to find them in broad areas. One might *differentiate* among various brands of bourbon, and at the same time *distinguish* bourbon from a chocolate malted. And the verb **discriminate** belongs in here, going *differentiate* one better, to pick up the smallest nuance of difference in detail and to convey not only ability but expertise. A doctor, deciding what pills to prescribe, may *discriminate* among them; his patient, deciding which of the pills to take, should *differentiate*. (He should also *distinguish* his pills from the cocker spaniel's.)

Yet the instant these verbs are used as nouns, so that *differentiate* becomes *difference* and *distinguish* becomes *distinction*, they swap roles! Now *distinction* is the one that goes to fine detail, while difference goes to the broader fields. When somebody tries to sidestep his way out of an argument by claiming some meaningless point of dissimilarity, we say, "That's a distinction without a difference." And surely most citizens know the *difference* (not the *distinction*— it's too broad for that) between good and evil.

diminish, minimize   To *diminish* is to reduce to some degree; to *minimize* is to reduce to the smallest possible degree. The difference here was accurately depicted by the late Dizzy Dean when he was asked if he thought the 1948 Chicago Cubs could win the pennant. "They have two chances," he said. "Slim and none."

disassociate, dissociate   Since both mean the same thing, both are right; yet *dissociate* is preferable. Any time you can make a word shorter without changing its meaning, its impact, even its sound, why not?

Will the same rule apply to **disassemble, dissemble**? It will not. These two are light years apart in meaning. To *disassemble* is to take apart. To *dissemble* is to put forth a false or concealing appearance.

disclose, divulge   *Divulging* is a less widespread act than *disclosing*. A politician might *disclose* his intent to run for office in a statewide announcement; that same day, his wife might *divulge* to her parents her intent to divorce him. Another word, *reveal*, is a pet of some headline and copy writers, but revelation ought to be saved for authentic miracles and for the magician who gets the woman out of the trunk.

discomfit, discomfort   See also the ensuing entry for **discreet, discrete**. The problem there is worse, because *discreet* and *discrete* are pronounced exactly the same, whereas the speaker can distinguish the *fit* sound from the *fort*. In meaning, to *discomfit* is to puzzle, perplex, disconcert; to *discomfort* is to make uncomfortable, deject.

discover, invent   To *invent* something is to originate it. To *discover* is to come across something that was already there. Columbus *discovered* America; he didn't invent it. Edison *invented* the light bulb. (And held it to his ear and said, "Hello? Hello?")

discreet, discrete   This is awful. The first means circumspect, judicious, prudent; the second means separate. But the two words have the identical sound, and to hear the sentence *Copies of these letters should be circulated discreetly to the eight partners*, leaves the listeners totally uninformed as to whether it was *discreetly* or *discretely* that was intended. Even seeing it in writing can be hazardous: *should be circulated discretely to the eight partners* can leave the suspicion that the writer meant *discreetly* but couldn't spell it.

One difference between the two words is that few people know *discrete* and even fewer use it. That still leaves them capable of misspelling *discreet* so it comes out *discrete*, and we're back at square one.

The burden is on the communicator to use *discrete* discreetly.

discriminate—see **differentiate**

disinterested, uninterested   One (*dis-*) means **impartial,** the other (*un-*) means **indifferent.** "An umpire, ideally, is disinterested," Roy Copperud writes; "one who does not care about the game is uninterested." And, from Edward Johnson, this advice: "These words have become so confused that it is often better to use *impartial, indifferent,* or some other word that still has a commonly understood precise meaning."

dissemble—see **disassociate**

distinguish—see **differentiate**

divide, separate   To *separate* is to set apart or keep apart, while to *divide* has more of the implication of rearrangement of an existing group, and an implication too of disagreement. *Divide* carries with it also the notion that the subgroups will be approximately equal in size. *Separating* the white clothes from the colored before doing the laundry simply means what it says, regardless of how many clothes there may be in each category. But to *divide* the clothes into separate categories implies the number of articles in each category is about the same.

divulge—see *disclose*

dominate, domineer   *Dominating* means strong, powerful; *domineering* smacks of the tyrant or bully. To quote from *A Dictionary of Contemporary American Usage*, "*Dominate*, sometimes, has unpleasant connotations. *Dominate* always has." Nice side: *For years the Empire State Building dominated the Manhattan skyline*. Ugly side: *Frankenstein's castle domineered the village*. Note the "towering above" image in both words.

donate, give, present   *Give* is the catch-all, the shortest, and the best. *Present* is fitting for formal occasions, but not necessary. *Donate* has the connotation of giving something free of charge—whether money, goods, or services—but here once again, *give* can do the job. Without presenting or donating too much thought to it, do give some thought to using *give* more, and *donate* and *present* less. There's an overformality, however unconsciously applied, to the last two.

   An added word about *present*: Without changing its spelling, it's sounded differently as a verb than as a noun, the accent shifting from the second to the first syllable, and the *e* going from long to short. Some other words have similar quirks. William Safire points out that *excuse* as a verb has a soft *s*, shifting to a hard *s* when it's used as a noun. And *entrance* the noun not only has a different sound but a different meaning from *entrance* the verb. For that matter, why are *core*, *lore*, *more*, and *pore* all pronounced the same, but *cost* and *lost* one way and *most* and *post* another? Don't look for the answer here.

   The mysteries of our language surround us. Although there is little glamour in the thought of journeying through the various sounds that pour from the diphthong *ou*, such a tour could give us a sentence like this one, which has 10 words containing *ou*—each with its own separate pronunciation. The noun *buffet* not only has different pronunciations for its different meanings—one when it means a blow with the hand, another when it means a sideboard or a spread of refreshments—but actually has to be listed twice in dictionaries just to account for its origins (the slap is Middle English, the eats are French).

And even words of one syllable can be pronounced in more than one way: *live*, depending on the form; *wind* or *lead*, depending on the meaning; and *read*, even though the meaning is the same!

doubt, doubtful *Doubtful* means more in doubt than *in doubt* does. In *We may be leading in the seventh inning, but victory is still in doubt*, we mean we're not sure of winning. If *victory is doubtful* it means we think we're likely to lose.

A similar shift in emphasis occurs when we follow *doubt* with *that*, instead of with *whether*. In Morton Freeman's example, "Uncertainty in 'They doubt *whether* he stole the money' becomes incredulity in 'They doubt *that* he stole the money.'"

In questions and in negative statements, *that* always follows *doubt*: *We don't doubt that you're giving a true account. . . . Do you doubt that I'm giving a true account?*

dreamed, dreamt The former is more in use in the United States, the latter in the British Isles, but there's more to it than that. The ear takes over on this one. For prosaic or unpleasant subjects, *dreamed* is better, while the fanciful and pleasant might more nicely take *dreamt*. The husband says: "I dreamt we won the lottery." The wife says: "I dreamed we didn't."

due to If you had to single out the one word misused by more people more often than any other, *due* would be a prime candidate, due to its use in the phrase *due to*. That's probably the most interesting thing that can be said about it. The misuse isn't fatal, not even serious, and certainly not all that fascinating to examine, rooted as it is in the arcane grammatical specifications distinguishing the adjective (which *due* in this context is) from the adverbial phrase or preposition (which it isn't). In any event, *Due to my dentist I was late for work* is just downright wrong. What's due to your dentist is payment of his bill. As the French say, *vive le dental plan*.

Of course there are proper ways to use *due to* (a good idea is to make sure it follows some form of the verb *to be*—*The postponement was due to rain* is correct); but there are other expressions, like *because of, on account of, owing to,* that serve just as well with far less risk of being misused. No more on this topic, due to space.

E

effect—see *affect*

effective, effectual, efficacious, efficient   *Effective*: Someone who produces good results, something that works (*an effective speaker, an effective remedy*); also something that's in operation (*the law became effective at midnight*). *Effectual*: First cousin to *effective,* but relating even more to change or success. A speech might be *effective* and still not win the audience over. An *effectual* speech will definitely win them over. *Efficient*: Much the same, but with the added flavor of saving space, money or time. *Efficacious*: Again the same thrust of meaning, but with two grace notes: (1) It's best used only after the desired result has been achieved (*That was* [not *That will be*] *an efficacious way of handling the matter*); and (2) *efficacious* is applied only to things, never to people.

egoist, egotist   Both are wrapped up in self, but *egoism* is a philosophy that says self-interest is the purpose of moral actions, and a given *egoist* might never discuss his beliefs with anyone. The *egotist* talks all the time, and boastfully so, about himself.

either . . . or / neither . . . nor   The rule says that the verb following *or* or *nor* in these constructions depends, for whether it's singular or plural, on its nearest antecedent. In *Neither the general nor his lieutenants were involved,* the verb *were* is plural because *lieutenants* is plural. In *Either John or Fred is already there waiting for you, is* is singular because so's *Fred.* But, in *Either John or his friends are already there,* the plural *friends* requires the plural *are.* And any later language in the sentence should conform: *Either John or Fred is already there in his office* (singular *is*, singular *his*, singular *office*); *Either John or his friends are already in their offices* (plural *are*, plural *their*, plural *offices*).

One thing about this rule: it's consistent. Thus, if we want to reverse John and his friends, then we have to say, "Either John's friends or John himself *is* already in *his office*," which the ear may think is absurd. But the rule demands it: The subject nearest to the verb is the singular *John himself*, requiring not only the singular *is* but the singular *his* and singular *office*.

And here we go again with the ladies: *Either John or Edith is already in his office* would obey the rule, yet not even the rulemaker would use it. It not only subjects Edith to gratuitous neglect, but raises the possibility that she occupies John's office instead of her own. Do we then make it, *Either John or Edith is already in his or her office?* That's even worse; now either one could be in either one's office. To make sense, we have to violate the rule, and the most sensible violation is *Either John or Edith are already in their offices*.

Best way to deal with this rule is probably to never have learned it (just as *to never have* is a blameless way to split an infinitive). You can say, "JFK is a little far, but either LaGuardia or Newark are fine," and who's going to come along and tell you *are fine* should have been *is fine?* Nobody.

elder, older The former can be applied only to persons, the latter to either persons or things. For expressions of more than two, **eldest** and **oldest** are used.

emigrant, immigrant We *emigrate from* and *immigrate to*, so if your great grandparents came from Europe, it's equally correct to say either they *emigrated from France* or *immigrated to California*. Or: *They immigrated to California from France/They emigrated from France to California*. One added note: You're an *emigrant* from the moment the move begins. You're not an *immigrant* till you get there.

endless, innumerable   Not the same. *Endless* means without end, *innumerable* means too many to count. Think of the treads on the down escalator at Bloomingdale's: they may be *endless* but they're hardly *innumerable*. In many cases, though, the words can be used interchangeably. If you have one brother-in-law who says he has endless problems, and another who says he has innumerable problems, both of them have problems.

endorse, indorse   No difference.

ensure—see *assure*

episode—see *accident*

equally   Do we use *as* before *equally*, as in *He was as equally unhappy with the Red Sox as he was with the Tigers*, or after, as in, *He was equally as unhappy with the Red Sox as he was with the Tigers?* The answer is, neither. The *as* is superfluous either place. (Fowler calls it "an illiterate tautology." So there.) *He was equally unhappy with the Red Sox as he was with the Tigers* is it. Point is, in this context *equally* already means *as*.

essential, substantial   These adjectives have clearly different meanings. *Essential* means someone or something that can't be done without; *substantial* refers to something significant. Thus, by virtue of his owning 45 percent of the stock, Mr. Blake can be said to have *substantial* influence on the fate of Company X, while Mrs. Blake, who owns no stock but tells Mr. Blake what to do, would have an *essential* influence on it.

  As the adverbs **essentially** and **substantially**, however, the two words become virtually interchangeable. There isn't really much difference between being *essentially* or *substantially* in disagreement with Mr. and Mrs. Blake. In this and similar contexts, though, *substantially* may be the stronger word. To say of Mr. Blake that "though now semi-retired, he's still *essentially* in charge," would mean he still has the name of boss. To make it ". . . he's still *substantially* in charge" means he's got the game as well as the name.

estimate, estimation These are used as interchangeable nouns and probably shouldn't be. *Estimation* takes longer to say, and so sounds more important, but it actually means "the forming of an estimate." That makes *estimate* the word people mean when they use *estimation*.

event—see *accident*

everyday, every day The first of these is an adjective. In *Rain is an everyday occurrence*, it describes the noun *occurrence*. For that reason it's spelled as a single word. But in *It rains every day*, it becomes an adverbial phrase telling how often it rains, and is two words.

exceptionable, exceptional Confusing these two words is not a good idea. *Exceptionable* applies to people only, and relates to something objectionable in word or deed. *Exceptional* can mean things as well as people, and it means unusual, extraordinary.

excuse As a noun, *excuse* should not be confused with *reason*. A *reason* is a reason, good, bad or indifferent. An *excuse* is at best a justification, at worst an alibi.

In using it as a verb, do you say "*Excuse* me" or do you say "*Pardon* me"? Unless you're in front of a judge or a parole board, a simple "Excuse me" ought to suffice.

F

facility, faculty The difference between these two isn't immense, except for situations where the restrooms for teachers at the university are a facility for the faculty. But when they're taken to mean aptitude or skill or capability, usually either one can be used. *Facility* has in it the flavor of something that comes easily to the practitioner, often something that has been taught by an outsider and developed through practicing, as in *a facility for playing the flute*. *Faculty* is more in the line of something you were born with, such as *a faculty for bumping into things*.

false comparison *The players on our team are not as tall as St. Ignatius.* How tall is St. Ignatius?

What's meant, of course, is that the players on the St. Ignatius team are taller than those on our team. Some words got left out. It should have been, *The players on our team are not as tall as those on St. Ignatius.*

Hasty writing often squeezes out the relative pronoun and preposition (like *those* and *on* above), and the so-called false comparison results. Sometimes it comes from the omission of the preposition alone, as in *Interest rates were two points lower than the same months last year*, which compares rates with months. It should be *lower than* in *the same*, so rates are compared with rates. A similar example, given by Roy Copperud, shows how ambiguity can result: "Personal income was up 8 percent last year, higher than any other state." As Copperud asks, was the increase or the income higher? It should have read, ". . . than *in* any other state."

farther, further *Farther* should be used for distance (*The farther from England, the nearer to France*), *further* for time or amount (*Ten minutes further into the recital, things got interesting. . . . We could use some further information*). But there are some instances when the two words are interchangeable, as when distance and time become one and the same: *Our new house will be 15 minutes further/farther from the city than the old one*—should it be *further* or *farther*? Nobody knows.

feasible, possible The difference here, Fowler points out, is that between something that is do-able and something likely to happen. A *possible* plan of action is one we can undertake; a *feasible* plan is one we can expect to execute successfully.

figuratively, literally *Literally* means literally following the letter or the exact word; *figuratively* applies to figures of speech, thus is applied to a manner of speaking. To say, "My heart literally stopped beating," raises the question of how you are still here to say anything at all. Would the remedy be to say, "My heart figuratively stopped beating?" Yes and no. Yes, in the sense that that's what you really mean; no, in the sense that the sentence is better off without either *literally* or *figuratively*. *Figuratively* is used seldom; even so, it is probably overused. *Literally* is used with great frequency, most often as a mistaken replacement for *figuratively*, and so is even more overused.

figure, number *Number* can be used for either the physical symbol of a number or for any other numerical expression. *Figure* should be used only for the physical symbol. Thus we can refer to *the figure 5 on the blackboard*, or speak of an ice skater completing a *figure 8*, but we would say, "The *number* (not *figure*) of people in the theater exceeded its seating capacity."

final completion There is no other kind. The *final* is unnecessary.

first—see *former*

firstly (*secondly, thirdly, etc.*) Try them without the *-ly* ending.

flammable, inflammable They mean exactly the same, although, as Harry Shaw says, "In referring to someone's temperament or behavior, *inflammable* seems more appropriate."

flaunt, flout Saying one of these when we mean the other may not be the greatest mistake in the language, but it's certainly one of the most frequently warned against. Small wonder, since—unlike *affect/effect* or *complement/compliment*—*flaunt* and *flout* don't sound alike, so there's no hiding place when you misuse them aloud. In any event, here goes *Webster's New Collegiate Dictionary*: to *flaunt* is to "wave or flutter showily . . . display ostentatiously"; to *flout* is to "treat with contemptuous disregard." Thus, *By flaunting his red sneakers he flouted the dress code*.

following When *following* is used to mean "after," it would be better to use *after*. (And when *frequently* is used to mean "often," which it always is, it would be better to use *often.*) Cf. Churchill's "Short words are best."

forgot, forgotten—see *got*

former, latter   These should be used only for expressions of two. In *History and calculus are taught; the former is the tougher course, former* is used correctly. But if history, calculus, and French are taught, history may still be the toughest, yet here we may not use *former.* Instead, we would say *the first* (or *the first of those,* or *the first-named,* or *the first of which,* or *the first of them*). Similarly, the second in a series of two takes *latter,* but the last of three or more takes *last.*

The rule on *former, latter* is first cousin to the rule that made us use *tougher* in the preceding paragraph where history and calculus—two subjects—were involved, but *toughest* when it became history, calculus, and French—three subjects. The comparative degree—*former, latter, tougher*—is for expressions of two; the superlative degree—*first, last, toughest*—for three or more. (Since *first* is also an adjective of number, it can be used that way in series of two, instead of *former,* just as *second* can be used instead of *latter.*)

The ruling having been given in this matter, the fact remains that wrong usage here sacrifices nothing in the way of clarity. To say, "Between John, George and Jim, the latter is my favorite," is to use *between* when you mean *among,* and *latter* when you mean *last,* but your meaning will be clear enough. So here we are talking not clarity but quality. There's something to be said for that too.

fortuitous, fortunate   It's surprising how often *fortuitous* is used when *fortunate* was meant. *Fortuitous* means accidentally, by chance. Unfortunately it also means lucky, so maybe it isn't surprising how often *fortuitous* is used when *fortunate* was meant. A bridge player might say that by a *fortuitous* stroke of luck, his partner held the ace. He could just as well say that by a *fortunate* stroke of luck, his partner held the ace. But if the opponents held the ace, that stroke of luck, while *fortuitous,* is hardly *fortunate.* In short, *fortunate* means fortunate; *fortuitous* can be either fortunate, unfortunate, or neither of those: it's totally impartial.

Frankenstein Next time you're tempted to say somebody "created a Frankenstein," you might want to remember that Frankenstein was the doctor who did the creating, not the monster created. On the other hand, you might not want to remember it. Another example of misuse gaining respectability through repetition.

frequently—see *following*

from whence *Whence* means from where, so *from whence* means from from where. Maybe *whence* should be jettisoned altogether (along with *whither*). Nobody goes around saying, "Whence did she come, whither is she going?" *Where did she come from, where is she going?* does it fine.

further—see *farther*

G

gay This has a connotation today that was unknown a generation ago, but that is the way language changes, and *gay* certainly is not the only word of this kind. Tradition has been altered because of it, as in the singing of "My Old Kentucky Home" with its line " 'Tis summer, the darkies are gay. . . ." Bye.

genius, talent Best definition of the difference between these two—if any definition is needed—may have arisen the night Oscar Levant, the pianist, and George Gershwin, the composer, found themselves occupying a Pullman compartment on an overnight train. To settle the question of who would sleep where, Gershwin pointed to Levant. "Talent in the upper berth," he said. Then he pointed to himself. "Genius in the lower."

There have been many definitions of *genius*: "Genius is only a great aptitude for patience." . . . "Genius is 1 percent inspiration and 99 percent perspiration." . . . "A genius is someone who does readily what no one else can do at all." A. Conan Doyle may have resolved something when he wrote, "Mediocrity knows nothing higher than itself, but talent instantly recognizes genius." And Thomas de Quincey really threw himself into it: "Talent and genius," he wrote, "are not merely different, they are in polar opposition to each other. Talent is intellectual power of every kind, which acts and manifests itself . . . through the will and the active forces. Genius . . . is that much rarer species of intellectual power which is derived from the genial nature—from the spirit of suffering and enjoying—from the spirit of pleasure and pain. It is a function of the passive nature." You tell 'em, Tom.

gerrymander The *g* is sounded as *j*, and thus the word often appears erroneously as *jerrymander*. We include it here not for that reason, but because of its fascinating derivation, of a kind that no other language but English can display. To quote from *A Dictionary of Contemporary American Usage*, "The word derives from Elbridge Gerry, one of the signers of the Declaration of Independence, a member of the Continental Congress and later of the Congress of the United States, twice governor of Massachusetts and, at the time of his death, vice-president of the United States. Despite this distinguished and honorable career, his name is fixed in the language through his connivance (in an unsuccessful attempt to get himself elected governor of Massachusetts for a third term) in a scheme to redistribute the electoral districts of the state in such a way that the strength of the party opposing him was concentrated in a few districts. Gilbert Stuart, the painter, seeing a map with the new districts marked on it, thought it resembled the body of an animal, added head, claws and wings and said it would do for a salamander. A gentleman present changed it to *gerrymander*, and the word stuck."

give—see **donate**

glance, glimpse A glance is the taking of a quick, passing look; a *glimpse* is the quick, passing sight of what's being looked at: *I only*

got a glance at the headline, but one glimpse was enough. So—
glance is what you give, *glimpse* is what you receive.

glutton, gourmand, gourmet   As opposed to those who eat to live, all
three of these live to eat. The *gourmet* has the most selective taste,
but swallows the least. The *glutton* can't tell one dish from another
and doesn't care, so long as there's a lot of it. The *gourmand* is
halfway between the other two. He has at least some ability to
distinguish between fine cuisine and garbage, but he also likes his
plate full.

gopher   A burrowing rodent, according to all dictionaries; but Stephen
Sondheim, a genius of the American musical theatre, began his
career as one, as did many of us lesser creatures: someone who
would *go for* coffee, *go for* the newspapers, *go for* sandwiches. Presto:
an additional meaning for an existing word. It's also spelled *gofer*,
and other words not yet recognized by dictionaries but similarly
utilizing the preposition *for* have been entering the language, most
notably *twofer*, a contraction of the concept of two-for-one. ("We
had a threefer last night," an intern at our local hospital said recently:
his way of reporting the birth of triplets.)

Within the first four typewritten pages of a magazine article I've
been writing—a retrospective piece about an event that happened
in 1961—I find I've used five different words or expressions that I
couldn't have used in 1961, simply because they didn't exist . . . not
in the form anyway that I was using them now. Yet all five have
become so commonplace in their new dress that I could use them
without a second thought.

Other entries in this book refer to usages that are being aban-
doned. But in most cases other usages are taking their place. In the
net the language keeps getting richer.

Nevertheless, a warning has been sounded here by David Melinkoff, a UCLA law school professor and author of several works
on the language of the law. He was speaking of law students (but
his words have broader application) who "hoard words like a squirrel
hoards nuts—without thinking what to keep and what to drop."

Melinkoff's warning was echoed by Dr. Lois DeBakey, of Baylor College of Medicine, who said that many doctors speak or write unintelligibly to hide muddled thinking or simply glamorize their profession. "Some of them write in a Latin, medieval style," she said, "because they fear it won't be valued enough if people understand it."

got, gotten   The word is *got*. As to *forgot, forgotten,* either one is acceptable.

grammar, syntax   These are often used loosely, with no harm done. *Grammar,* to give it careful definition, has to do with the relationship of words to one another. *Syntax* deals with the order in which words appear. If *grammar* were the main office, *syntax, spelling, punctuation* and *pronunciation* would be the branch offices.

grow   We might say, "See how our baby has grown." We'd never say, "See how we've grown our baby." Or wouldn't we?

Just in the past couple of years, something horrible has been happening to *grow. We want to make our company grow* is now, more and more, *We want to grow our company.* Time was we grew asparagus, onions, and old. Now we're growing all sorts of things: problems, deficits, interest payments, the size of our work force, bus schedules, production, prices at the gas pump, dental treatments, vacation time, you name it.

Grow as a transitive verb (one that takes a direct object) should be limited to processes of natural generation: *I grow nasturtiums, you grow peonies, the dog is growing a new coat, the glaciers grew a crust.* It should not be used in place of *increase* or *expand,* unless the sense is intransitive, as in *The troubles of the English language are growing,* which they obviously are.

H

habitable, inhabitable The first of these refers to dwellings—housing for people, trees or dens or burrows for animals; the second to cities or countries or other large areas. The verb in both cases is *inhabit*. The negative adjective in both cases is *uninhabitable*.

half A complicated word, being at once a noun (*my better half*), an adjective (*half the world*), an adverb (*half past six*), and, though the spelling is obsolete, a verb (today we use *halve* instead). One question concerns the plural—when do we say *halves*, when *half*? Best policy here is to use *half* when talking about general or abstract things, *halves* in terms of specific objects. Thus we would *cut the apples in halves*, while because there is so little time left we'll *cut the arguments in half*.

hanged, hung People are *hanged*, other animals and objects are *hung*. Webster's Third and others now say *hung* is okay for people too. Not by me it's not. I had an editor once who changed it on me, turning a man being hanged into a man being hung. What nettled me was not so much that he was turning something right into something wrong but that he bothered to make such a meaningless change to begin with. The late, great Theodore Bernstein of *The New York Times* said the inner ring of hell was reserved for editors who overedit. The innermost ring was for those who overedit and make it wrong. If anybody cares, I intend to go to my reward being hanged, not hung.

heir apparent/presumptive The *heir apparent* has it better. Soon as the uncle, or whoever, kicks off, the inheritance becomes reality. An *heir presumptive* will get the inheritance assuming nothing goes wrong. He or she might inherit only if the ancestor dies before—or after—1994. Or only if no male child is born between now and then. Or whatever *if* might apply.

historic, historical *Historic* means history-making. *Historical* pertains to the study of the subject of history. *No historical review of World War II can ignore the historic landing in Normandy.*

hopeless—see *desperate*

hyphen The hyphen is used less and less to separate words or parts of words. What once were bi-focals now are bifocals; what used to mis-fire now misfires; what once was un-used is now unused; smokers have become nonsmokers; but so have non-smokers. Common adverbs ending in *-ly* once were commonly hyphenated, as in *widely-understood*, but these days the equally widely understood premise is that they go without the hyphen. When the adverb has the same adjectival standing as the adjective it describes, or when two adjectives are used as a unit, the hyphen still should appear—for clarity's sake. Somebody might think a hot tempered lady was both hot and tempered, when what's meant, of course, is hot-tempered. But hot running water, in contrast, gives us two quite separate descriptions of the water: it's running and it's hot. So we would never say "hot-running." Hot unhyphenated running water will do.

When a noun is used as an adjective (*He is a city boy*—i.e., a boy from the city), no hyphen is required. But if that noun in turn is preceded by an adjective, the hyphen would come into play depending on the intended meaning. A *big city boy* is a boy from the city who is big. A *big-city* boy is a boy from a big city. Clarity is really the sole goal of the hyphen, unless you are a producer-director or producer-director-writer or cameraman-actor, in which case it's simply a connective convenience (your guild will officially call you a "hyphenate"). For clarity's sake, use the hyphen if 20-odd senators showed up at your party (without the hyphen, you hosted 20 oddballs from the Senate). And if Horowitz and O'Rourke have a Toyota dealership, make them Japanese-car dealers. Without the hyphen, Horowitz and O'Rourke just became Japanese. (If they also sell used cars, then as Fowler puts it, "A little used car is not necessarily the same as a little-used car.")

hypothecate, hypothesize

Just as with prefixes, suffixes that once followed a hyphen now more and more are used just as a continuation of their words. What used to be *life-like* became *lifelike* (for that matter, *lifelike-ness* has become *lifelikeness*), and indeed, what once was *life-style* turned into *life style*, and today is *lifestyle*. But *bull-like* is still *bull-like*, the alternative being *bulllike* (the "l" key got stuck?). And a man named Tucker from Philadelphia (no relation, we will guess, to the Tucker of Tucker's Law), wrote to William Safire complaining about "the most egregious nonhyphenation" favored by *The New York Times*. The reference was to a typical headline in the society pages using the word "rewed," as in "MRS. SMITH REWED." "It leads to meditations along the line of, 'She rewed the day she met him,' or 'Why was he so rewed to her?' " Tucker wrote. Safire, for his part, has his own rule for the hyphen: "When in doubt, leave it out, unless it looks funny."

hypothecate, hypothesize   I had an English teacher in high school who said, "Use a word three times and it's yours." He meant, of course, using it correctly. I used to say "hypothecate" when I meant "hypothesize." Peter Griffin of the department of mathematics at Sacramento State University corrected me. Six years later I did the same thing, and Larry Newman of Manning, Selvage & Lee corrected me. What my English teacher failed to realize was that if once is an accident, twice is a habit. And three times is a pleasure.

My problem was that something in my head told me *hypothecate* and *hypothesize* meant essentially the same thing, and my ear preferred the sound of "hypothecate." It still does. The sad thing is they don't mean the same at all. To *hypothesize* is to express a hypothesis, a proposition or principle, a supposition or conjecture put forth to account for known facts. To *hypothecate*, on the other hand, is, of all things, to pawn, to mortgage, to give as pledge or security. "Trust the ear," Roy Copperud advises in his *Webster's Dictionary of Usage and Style*. He's right, without question. Ninety-nine percent of the time.

Within this confessional, let me also bring up the word *magistry*.

There's a word with a sound to it! I used it in a television script, to invoke the image of the umpire in baseball, combining perfectly as it does the sense both of majesty and magistrate. Here everyone accepted it—William Conrad, who narrated the show; Lee Mendelson, who produced it; AT&T, which sponsored it; CBS, which ran it. About two years later I made an accidental discovery: there is no such word.

Trust the ear. Ninety-nine percent of the time.

I

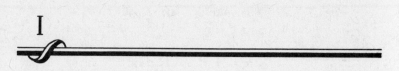

idea—see *concept*

illegal, illicit, unlawful *Illegal* is the one with the narrowest meaning; it applies only to what is prohibited by statutory law. *Unlawful* can also mean *illegal*, but it is broader, and could apply to church law or even the by-laws of an organization or the rules of a company. *Illicit* is the broadest of the three, and can be used for anything that goes against custom or authorization. *Illicit* also has in it the flavor of thievery or stealth. In this day and age, adultery may no longer be *illegal*, and only some people would refer to it any longer as *unlawful*, but it still qualifies as an *illicit* relationship.

illegible, unreadable *Illegible* means it literally can't be read. *Unreadable* could mean illegible, but it also could mean too boring or complex to read.

immigrant—see *emigrant*

impartial—see *disinterested*

incessant—see *continual*

incident—see *accident*

inconceivable, unthinkable *Inconceivable* describes that which the mind cannot imagine; *unthinkable* is something no decent person would do or allow to be done—but somebody will probably think of it.

inconsequent, inconsequential In today's usage, *inconsequent* denotes that which is irrelevant or illogical; *inconsequential*, which used to mean the same thing, now describes that which is trivial, unimportant.

indifferent—see ***disinterested***

indorse—see ***endorse***

inexecrable Speaking of nonwords, here's another one. Difference between this one and *magistry* is that some dictionaries do carry *inexecrable*, if only for the sake of calling it, as the Oxford does, "a misprint." Yet people do use the word frequently enough for authorities like the Oxford to take notice of it.

What, then, do people mean when they say "inexecrable"? A *Dictionary of Problem Words and Expressions* theorizes that it is "probably mistaken for some such word as *inexorable*." Equally likely is the notion that people say "inexecrable" in place of *execrable*, which means abominable, detestable. *Inexecrable* does have a zazzy ring to it, as nonwords go.

inexpensive—see ***cheap***

infantile—see ***childish***

infectious—see ***contagious***

infer, imply *Imply* is what you put into it, *infer* is what you get out of it: *I infer from what you imply that you are thinking of suing me for giving bad advice.*

inflammable—see ***flammable***

inform—see ***advise***

inhabitable—see ***habitable***

innumerable—see ***endless***

insure—see ***assure***

intend—see *design*

invent—see *discover*

ironic, sarcastic, sardonic, satiric   Few among us have not used one of these words; even fewer have not used one when they meant one of the other three.

Ironic means the opposite of, or at least something other than, what is expressed. Saying "Nice game!" to a shortstop who made three errors in one inning is being ironic. It is also being *sarcastic*. But there is this difference: *ironic* does not have to be mean-spirited, intended to be injurious. If it's raining like crazy, and you say, "What a lovely day!"—that's irony, not sarcasm: it doesn't do injury to anybody. Sarcasm, on the other hand, is meant to wound or mock. Also, it is hard to be *sarcastic* when describing oneself (a seldom-used but better word there would be **mordant**). But *irony* can be either inward- or outward-directed.

Sardonic is very like sarcastic, but is reserved most often to describe features or actions, rather than words or people. Thus a *sarcastic* remark may be accompanied by a *sardonic* laugh or grin.

Satiric means the mocking of a work already in place, like a performance or a body of words or pictures. The object of satire must pre-exist: if Melville had never written *Moby Dick*, no one could satirize it. One of the prominent satirists of our time, Andy Warhol, won acclaim with a simple and accurate drawing of a can of Campbell's tomato soup. This was called—perhaps ironically— "pop art."

(What, then, is **parody**? A parody can be satiric in intent, if not always in result, and may not be intended as such at all. A poor imitation of something could be described as a parody. And when we say "parody" we almost inevitably mean a written composition.)

irregardless   There is no such word. The word is *regardless*.

irritate—see *aggravate*

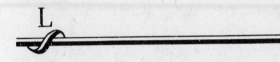

J

join together Since *join* already means to unite or connect, the *together* is hardly necessary. There are some other equally common examples of redundancy in this book. My own favorite, not mentioned elsewhere because we don't run into it that often, is the case of *au jus*, which is French for *with juice*. This is sometimes found not only on American menus but in American conversation as *with au jus*, meaning *with with juice*, which is doubly redundant, using an extra language to express an extra *with*.

L

last, latest It can be argued that instead of the usual three degrees, the adjective *late* has four: *late, later, latest* and *last*. At times, there can be confusion between the last two: *latest* means the most recent, but *last* can mean most recent or final or both. Does *The last issue of our monthly newsletter came out a week ago* mean the most recent issue was also the final issue? A prudent way to avoid such confusion is to use only *latest* for recency and only *last* for finality.

Meanwhile, when *late* is used to mean deceased, watch out for redundancy. In *widow of the late . . .*, *widow* has already told us the man is no longer living.

How long should people have been dead before we stop using *late* to describe them? There's no fixed rule here, because *late* means living until recently, and everyone has a different definition of what's recent. *I haven't seen you lately* could mean two weeks or two years, depending, among other things, on how regularly we were accustomed to seeing each other. In some cases, particularly when the audience doesn't know a death occurred, *late* can stretch back 25 years or more, as in an engagement notice on the society page in which Geraldine Smith, daughter of Mrs. Katherine Smith and the late Harvey M. Smith, is going to marry somebody. For all we know, Harvey died in 1958.

latter—see *former*

lay, lie   Let *sleeping dogs lie*, runs the old proverb, but no one nowadays will do that. "Your beard just lays there," says the LectricShave commercial. Everything we hear is *lays*, *lay* and *laying*. Good plain English is fighting a losing battle here, and it's one place where at least some of us ought to fight back. You *lay* something, but if the verb doesn't have an object, then you *lie*. *Lay* is transitive (it takes an object); *lie* is intransitive (it doesn't). To quote Strunk and White in *The Elements of Style*, "The hen, or the play, *lays* an egg; the llama *lies* down. The playwright went home and *lay* down." Principal parts, if you *lie* on the floor, are *lie* for the present tense . . . *lay* for the past tense . . . *had lain* for the past perfect . . . and *lying* for the participle or gerund. If you *lay* the book on the floor, principal parts are *lay* for the present tense . . . *laid* for the past . . . *had laid* for the past perfect . . . and *laying* for the participle or gerund. The idea of "principal parts" (all verbs have them) speaks for itself.

legitimize   From the adjective *legitimate*, meaning conformation with legal or other prevailing standards, come three verbs, all sounding and meaning the same—*legitimate*, *legitimatize*, and *legitimize*. The last is preferable.

lend, loan   Traditional English says that *lend* is the verb and *loan* is the noun, so that while we may ask the bank to give us the loan of some money, we must never ask the bank to loan us money. But *loan* has come into use as a verb, and most grammarians approve the usage.

More about this? Yes: When *loan* finally won approval as a verb, it was taken as automatic that its past tense was *loaned*. But—almost as an apology for having violated *lend*'s exclusivity as a verb—the past tense of *lend*, which is *lent*, now is used to go with *loan* as well. So we can say, "The bank promised to *loan* me some money, and in fact it *lent* me the full amount I asked for."

The fact remains that the ear wouldn't appreciate "Friends, Romans, countrymen, *loan* me your ears." A good idea is to preserve the earlier distinction, and use *loan* only as a noun.

lessee, lessor—see **mortgagor**

let alone *"This kind of incident has never happened in our city, let alone anywhere in the country,"* the police chief said. The chief may have been right, but he said it wrong. The right way was . . . *anywhere in the country, let alone in our city.* . . .

People do have a way of confusing what goes on which side of *let alone*. In fact, the chief could have been saying it right in the example above, except that it was taken from a newspaper story whose context made it wrong.

The phrase *let alone* is a means to heighten a point already made, through use of illustrative comparison. And the rule is that the point already made *follows* the *let alone*.

Thus:

Primary point: *My brother won't eat that kind of food.*
Follow-up comparison: *Neither will the entire Navy.*
Correct result: *The entire Navy wouldn't eat the food, let alone my brother.*

Note that in that example, as in the corrected version of the police chief's remarks, the smaller of the two entities being compared was what followed *let alone*. But that is accidental. What governs is the primary point, as in:

Primary point: *The Navy won't eat that food.*
Follow-up comparison: *My brother wouldn't either.*

Correct result: *My brother wouldn't eat that food, let alone the Navy.*

lie—see *lay*

literally—see *figuratively*

logic The use of logic as a force in effective communicating is not always what it's cracked up to be. This assertion may come as a surprise to some, but think of the times you've tried logic and it hasn't worked. An old-time couplet says, "A man convinced against his will/ Is of the same opinion still." And Jack Douglas, the humorist, recalled the time he was 12 years old and entered a contest requiring him to complete the sentence "I like Kellogg's because . . ." in 25 words or fewer. First prize was a football. Douglas wrote, "I like Kellogg's because I want a football." The logic was impeccable. He did not win.

(This is a good place for the double negative. To say or write, "I think I'm being logical in believing such-and-such," may have just a tinge of arrogance to it. Make it, "I hope I'm not being illogical . . ." and you've gentled it, made it a shade friendlier and more reasonable-sounding.)

Surely none of this can be taken as an indictment of logical thought per se. But sometimes a deeper logic takes hold, and—as seen in campaigns for political office—the art of persuasion often favors other means of approach. The title and opening line of one of our most beloved songs is "When I Grow Too Old to Dream." Years after he wrote it, the lyricist Oscar Hammerstein II described that as the most illogical line he ever wrote. "When do we grow too old to dream?" he said. "The line just doesn't make any sense." Somebody asked him if he was sorry he'd written it. "No," Hammerstein said.

M

majority, plurality A *majority* is more than half; a *plurality* is the highest among three or more contestants or numbers. Thus if in a three-candidate race I receive 34 votes and each of the two others gets 33, I won with a plurality of one vote and nobody had a majority; unless there were more than 200 registered voters, in which case the majority stayed home.

masterful, masterly The main quality of *masterful* is dominance; the main quality of *masterly* is skill. Someone who played a *masterly* game of tennis could still have lost the match to a *masterful* opponent.

maxim—see *motto*

mean—see *average*

media To say the media is interested in a piece of news is incorrect. Media *are*, not *is*. The word *media* came in with television, a medium for distributing news, advertising, sports, entertainment, etc. The printed word is another medium, often subdivided among newspapers, magazines, books. Radio is another. What started out being called a "press conference" became a "news conference" and today has even become a "media conference," all by way of reminding newspapers they're not the only ones with reporters. It's fun to note, though, how regularly the reminders forget: "press conference" is a phrase that has refused to die.

median—see *average*

militate, mitigate There is a *flaunt/flout* syndrome here . . . the wrongful using of one of the words when what's intended is the other. One difference is that *militate* takes *against*. It means to have weight or effect, and comes out reading, typically, like the sample in Webster's Second International—*His boyish appearance mili-*

tated against his getting an early promotion. Mitigate doesn't take *against* or anything else. It means to lessen, to cause to become less harsh or hostile. *His anger was mitigated by outside factors* means the anger was reduced. Thus, the familiar phrase, *mitigating circumstances.*

minimize—see *diminish*

mnemonic device   You're out in your boat on a dark night and you see the red and green running lights of another boat. How can you tell if it's moving toward you or away from you? Hazily, you remember that red is for the port side and green for starboard . . . or is it the other way around? And for that matter, when it comes to port and starboard, which is left and which is right?

To the rescue comes this table:

Left	Right
Port	Starboard
Red	Green

That tells us the red light belongs to the left, or port, side . . . and the green to the right, or starboard.

But wait: If we can't even allocate the individual words, what possible good does it do us to memorize the table? The answer is that we don't memorize the table. All we need to remember is that the shorter word always means the left side: just as *left* is shorter than *right*, so *port*, meaning left, is shorter than *starboard*, meaning right; and so *red*, denoting the left side, is shorter than *green*, denoting the right side.

The foregoing describes a *mnemonic device.* It comes from *Mnemosyne*, the Greek goddess of memory. You doubtless have several phrases or conceptions of your own, kept available in the back of your head, to help nudge memory. "Spring forward, fall back," the saying that reminds us which way to turn our clocks and watches to go on Daylight Saving Time in April, then back to Standard in October, is a most familiar mnemonic device.

It's intriguing to think of the words we have that come from proper names, such as *mnemonic*, or the more common *boycott*, *maverick*, or *gerrymander* (q.v.). On the other hand, far more proper names come from words: Smith, Carpenter, Farmer, etc. Equally intriguing, and more to the point, are the number of mnemonic devices that need their own mnemonic devices to be remembered properly.

mobile, movable *Mobile* refers to somebody or something that can move; *movable* to somebody or something that can be moved.

modern, modernistic At times these two words are synonymous, but where *modern* means anything that characterizes the times and styles of today, *modernistic* smacks more of the affected and the overblown.

mordant—see *ironic*

mortgagor, mortgagee The *mortgagor* is the buyer, the *mortgagee* the seller. This is the exact opposite of *lessor, lessee*. If you rent the apartment or house you live in, you're the *lessee*, and your landlord is the *lessor*.

motto, slogan A *motto* and a *slogan* can be one and the same, but a *slogan* has come to be associated more with advertising and promotion, usually encountered in written form, while a *motto* may have a loftier purpose, and seldom plays on words. Thus "When it rains it pours" is the clever *slogan* of a salt manufacturer, while "Be prepared" is the *motto* of the Boy Scouts.

Another word here is **maxim**, which is a general truth, fundamental principle, or rule of conduct, and therefore is more closely related to **proverb** than to either *motto* or *slogan*.

multilateral—see *bilateral*

N

naked, nude   Naked has the sexier connotation. The models in *Hustler* magazine are *naked*. The models in art class are *nude*.

name game   This is nothing more nor less than fun with words. You suit the name to the occupation, or vice versa, like:

Tattletale Gray—Confederate spy

Julian Alps—Yugoslavian mountain climber

Third Degree Burns—sadistic private detective

. . . or, putting the occupation first:

impotent philosopher—Immanuel Kant

   Make up your own list. Beyond being fun in and of itself, it's a state of relishing your own language. That's something good communicators have in common.

nauseated—see *contagious*

nauseous—see *contagious*

nearly, almost   Many grammarians have made subtle distinctions between these two words, at times imputing a positive nature to *nearly* that turns negative in *almost*, but they are so nearly alike that almost any choice you make will be the right one—except in this sentence, where *nearly*, used with *alike*, expresses physical proximity, while *almost*, used with *any choice*, goes to the metaphysical, the abstract. Thus: *I was nearly there before I realized I'd almost forgotten her name* uses *nearly* for geography, *almost* for thought.

   Yet the more you think about it, *I was almost there before I realized I'd nearly forgotten her name* is just as good. In fact, the ear likes it even better: *nearly forgotten her name* has a nicer sound to it. There's metaphysics for you!

notion—see *concept*

nude—see *naked*

number—see *figure*

O

occur, take place   There is more of the expected in *take place*, more of the unexpected, the unscheduled, in *occur*. Thus: *The incident occurred less than an hour before the trial was to* take place.

odds-on favorite   People use this expression all the time to denote a heavy favorite. If a horse in a race is favored at odds of 3-to-2, and no other horse in the race is better than 4-to-1, the 3-to-2 horse is obviously the heavy favorite. But he's *not* the odds-on favorite. He becomes that only when the odds are less than even money, such as 4-to-5 or 1-to-2.

The language of odds and percentages generally is subject to carelessness. The odds against rolling a seven at the crap table are 5-to-1, meaning we have one chance out of six. The house will pay you 4-to-1 if you do it. That's how the house makes money.

In casinos here and there, however, the payoff may be 5-for-1. How does the house make money that way?

The answer to that is that if you put up one dollar, and the house pays off at 4-to-1, you wind up with five dollars—your dollar plus the four the house paid you. At 5-for-1, you still wind up with five dollars—the house pays you five dollars, but keeps your one dollar. Odds of 4-*to*-1 and 5-*for*-1 are the same.

As for percentages, a candidate who defeats his opponent by getting 51 percent of the vote often is said to have squeaked in by one percentage point. A landslide it's not, but 51 percent means a margin of two percentage points, not one. If you got 51 percent in a two-candidate election, your opponent had to get 49. Either that or it was a funny election.

Percentages of increase and decrease also need to be handled with care. A price that goes from $8 one day to $10 the next reflects a 25-percent increase. But from $10 to $8 would be only a 20-percent decrease. The change was $2 in each case. But an increase is something that happens to a figure that goes up, as $8 went to $10, and $2 is 25 percent of $8. A decrease refers to the figure that went down, as $10 went to $8, and $2 is 20 percent of $10.

often—see *following*

only   In his book *Write to the Point,* John Stahr takes the sentence *I hit him in the eye yesterday* and diagrams it as follows:

(a) I (b) HIT (c) HIM (d) IN THE (e) EYE (f) YESTERDAY (g)

It was an exercise in seeing how many ways the word *only* could be placed in the sentence, and how the meaning changed. Stahr's translations:

(a) nobody else hit him; (b) I didn't scratch or bite him or anything else; (c) I didn't hit anybody else; (d) no other part of his anatomy was struck; (e) poor guy had only one, and I hit him in it! (f) as recently as yesterday; (g) not day before yesterday, or any other day, just yesterday.

It's good to give a little thought to where *only* belongs in any sentence; and even more when the phrasing *not only . . . but* is used to describe two separate actions. *We not only agreed to play them but we won* is correct. *We agreed not only to play them but we won* is not only incorrect, but doubly so. First, *only* modifies the infinitive *to play,* so the *but* should be followed by another infinitive, either *to beat them* or *to win.* And second, it's easy to believe we agreed to play them, but did we also agree to beat them?

oxymoron   This is the name for the rhetorical device of putting an adjective ahead of a noun it contradicts. *Hopeful pessimist, cruel kindness, friendly enemies* are examples, and it's a nice way of making a point. In an appearance some years back on Dick Cavett's television show, Dr. Henry Steele Commager, the historian, used "military intelligence" as another example, except that when he called it "an oxymoron," Cavett thought he was saying "a Nazi moron," which is not an oxymoron at all.

P

palpable, tangible   Both are defined as "capable of being touched." But *tangible* has in it a touch more of the real or material. Someone tells a falsehood and we call it, "A *palpable* lie," meaning it's such a blatant untruth we might figuratively reach out and touch it. To refute what was said, we might produce a book or set of figures as *tangible* proof that it was indeed a lie.

parody—see *ironic*

party   The use of this word to mean a person dates to the 17th Century. It fell into disuse, then experienced a rebirth in the United States around half a century ago when many telephone subscribers shared party lines, and phone operators referred to individuals by that label. But many people are, at least subconsciously, offended by being so addressed, and the word should be avoided.

people, persons   *People* is by now a readily accepted plural for *person*, and to say "There were two *people* at the door," sounds better than "There were two *persons* at the door." As for the plural of *people*, it is a word that is both singular and plural to begin with. Correct is *The Irish are a great people*, even though *are* is plural and *a* is singular! Equally correct is *The Irish and the Norwegians are two great peoples*. In fact, we have to say it that way. To say "The Irish and the Norwegians are two great *people*" is to sound as though we are describing only two *persons*.

perpetually—see *continual*

persuade—see *convince*

pinch hitter At a *ballpark guess*, the sport of baseball has probably contributed more to our everyday language than any other single source. Everybody knows somebody who's a *foul ball*, or *out of his league*, or who *never got to first base*, or is *out in left field*, or was *born with two strikes on him*. Even people who've never seen a baseball game (there are one or two) will use expressions like *hit-and-run*, *rain check*, *here's the pitch*, *crossed me up*, *get in there and pitch*, *got shut out*, *put one over*, *go to bat for*, *boot* (as a verb), *assist* (as a noun), *playing the percentages*, *close call*, *screwball*, *ground rules*, *going by the book*, and *touched all the bases*. (Describing a managing editor he once worked for, Morton Thompson wrote, "He reached puberty but forgot to touch second.") The list goes on and on: *warming up*, *holdout*, *threw me a curve*, *hardball*, *big league*, *bush league*, *keep swinging*, *circus play*, *grandstand play*, *double/triple play*, *old pro*, *cleanup man*, *big hitter*, *play-by-play*, *rhubarb*, *the big time*, *rookie*, *right off the bat*, *nothing/anything/something/plenty on the ball*, *bench-warmer*, *Ladies' Day*, *squeeze play*, *play ball*, *safe at home*, *pull a fast one*, and so on.

Even those phrases taken by baseball from other fields—*doubleheader* (railroading), *around the horn* (sailing), *grand slam* (bridge) and *pinch hitter* (the *pinch* comes from "How much can you raise in a pinch?" which in turn was the bartender's way of getting paid by miners whose money was the gold dust carried in a purse)— have rebounded into public use with baseball coloration.

Pinch hitter indeed has rebounded back out of baseball with still another coloration. Like *under par*, from golf, it means in general use the opposite of its baseball meaning. *Under par* in golf is good, in other things bad. The pinch hitter in baseball is a superior substitute; in other walks of life, barely equal if not inferior.

We even hear baseball where none was intended. The story is

told of a German traveler, arriving at Boston's Logan Airport and greeting the customs inspector with "Mein Herr, was sagst du?" "They lose, 8 to 5," the inspector said.

And that's the ball game.

plan—see *design*

plurality—see *majority*

possible—see *feasible*

practically, virtually The *Dictionary of Problem Words and Expressions* says, "*Practically* means *virtually* the same thing as *virtually*," and that's true enough, since both words mean our old friends *nearly, almost.*

But *practically* has an additional meaning, stemming from *practical*—realistic, effective. Looking at it *practically*, ain't no way the Seattle Mariners can win this year.

precipitate, precipitous Some words with a common root, like these from the Latin, nevertheless can take on wildly different meanings. Where *precipitate* means rash or headlong, *precipitous* means steep.

prescribe, proscribe Two more words from the Latin, again with totally different definitions. To *prescribe* is to order, to *proscribe* is to forbid.

present—see *donate*

presently Some purists insist that *presently* means soon, and only that. But it also means now, and if presently the purists don't know this, then presently they'll find out. There is, however, a chance for some ambiguity in using it both ways, as the preceding sentence might suggest. So, if not for purity's sake then for clarity's, a good idea is to use another word or phrase, such as *currently* or *at present*, when we mean now, and save *presently* for soon.

presume—see *assume*

preventative, preventive See the earlier entry where *legitimize* is preferred over *legitimatize*. Same thing here: We say ta-ta to the *at* and use the shorter word.

previously to   It's better to say *previous to* than *previously to*, because of the duplication factor. *Previous to* is an adverbial phrase, and *previously* is an adverb, so *previously to* uses the adverbial form twice where once is enough.

principal, principle   Strong challengers to the title of most often confused. *Principle* is a noun only, and it means a doctrine, a rule, a predetermined course of action. *Principal* is both a noun, meaning a sum of money, a chief person or main participant, and an adjective, meaning primary, foremost, main. *The* principal *of the school, a man of* principle, *regarded correct student behavior as one of his* principal *goals.*

Here is one more instance where no error can be detected in the spoken words, since they have an identical sound. It is in writing that the mistake shows itself, and even there it's hard to know whether the writer misunderstood the word, or understood it perfectly and simply spelled it wrong.

proscribe—see **prescribe**

proverb—see **motto**

prurient   Some people divine the word *pure* when they see or hear *prurient*. Too bad, since *prurient* means virtually the opposite of *pure*: lewd, possessed of lascivious thoughts or desires.

qualitative, quantitative   It's surprising how often these two get mixed up. *Qualitative* has to do with qualities, properties, characteristics; *quantitative* deals with quantities, numbers, volume. A *quantitative* analysis of this book might deal with the number of words and expressions it covers. A *qualitative* analysis would go to how it's written.

question mark   "Now, isn't it time you visited our Sales Pavilion and Model Park, and let our success story be yours." That happens to be a direct quote from a real estate ad in a newspaper, but you've read hundreds of others like it. What they have in common is that they ask a question but forget the question mark.

The writer of the sentence quoted above could argue that the ending of the sentence—". . . let our success story be yours"— doesn't have to be read as a question at all, so why follow it with a question mark? That argument won't hold. Any sentence that spins off an interrogative verb ought to end with a question mark.

Would you believe how many people don't recognize this fact! Wrong again: the exclamation point should have been a question mark! *Would you believe* launches a question, and the punctuation should reflect that fact.

Certainly neither of the examples given here suffers any loss of clarity for not being punctuated correctly, but something else can happen: All too often, the person reading your letter will note, even if subconsciously, that the expected question mark wasn't there, and that can affect the reaction to your entire message: however subtly, your power of expression can come into doubt.

Speaking of real estate ads, I have in front of me a letter from a condominium builder to his buyers which says, "All correspondence should be in writing." That is a good idea. Still another good idea, since this is about question marks, might be to get back to the subject. One final word: Don't use it in parentheses to be cute or ironical. The usage should be limited to times when there is genuine doubt about accuracy. *They have bought a nice (?) house in the suburbs* is wrong. *I am told the company has 23,000 (?) employees* is okay.

quotation marks   Not everything that is spoken has to be put inside quotation marks. *I asked him and he said no* is every bit as good as *I asked him and he said, "No." I tell you I expect your report immediately* is infinitely better than *I tell you, "I expect your report immediately."*

"The quotation mark is hopelessly overworked," Roy Copperud has said, and he makes special mention of fragmentary quotes such as *The victim's condition was reported as "good"* or *Some "swapping" may be necessary.* "Nothing is gained by quoting minor fragments like these, and the quotation marks clutter things up," Copperud says. "They also interfere with readability, for the reader necessarily pauses at a fragmentary quote to decide why the quotation marks are there. If this becomes too confusing, he may give up."

Edward Johnson agrees. "Quotation marks can be used to set off unfamiliar terms, nicknames, and words used in a peculiar way," he writes, "but this use can be overdone." And Geoffrey Nunberg makes reference to "the mania for quotation marks," citing a sign he saw in the window of a shoe-repair shop: WE ARE "CLOSED."

Some writers, Fowler says, put certain expressions in quotes to safeguard their own dignity. These writers put a slang phrase in quotes "because it suits them, & box the ears of people in general because it is slang; a refinement on the institution of whipping boys, by which they not only have the boy but do the whipping."

One other thing to be said on this subject is that when people are quoted, care should be taken to quote them correctly. The writer of fiction has an obvious advantage here; as John Updike puts it, "No character refuses to speak the lines we give him."

R

reasonable—see *cheap*

regret, repent To *regret* is to feel sorry about something you *or somebody else* has said or done. But one can only *repent* one's own words or behavior—and then do something about it. More sinners regret than repent.

reiterate If you've said something once and you now say it again, you aren't *reiterating*. You're *iterating*. From the third time on, you're reiterating.

replica—see *copy*

rhythm As a young man, somewhere between 1828 and 1830, Alfred Tennyson wrote a poem called "The Song of the Three Sisters" whose metric scheme was entirely new. Its first stanza goes:

The Golden Apple, the Golden Apple, the hallow'd fruit,
Guard it well, guard it warily,
Singing airily,
Standing about the charmed root,
Round about all is mute,
As the snowfield on the mountain peaks,
As the sandfield at the mountain foot.
Crocodiles in briny creeks
Sleep and stir not; all is mute.
If ye sing not, if ye make false measure,
We shall lose eternal pleasure,
Worth eternal want of rest.
Laugh not loudly: watch the treasure
Of the wisdom of the West.
In a corner wisdom whispers. Five and three
(Let it not be preach'd abroad) make an awful mystery:
For the blossom unto threefold music bloweth;
Evermore it is born anew,
And the sap in threefold music floweth,
From the root,
Drawn in the dark,
Up to the fruit,
Creeping under the fragrant bark,
Liquid gold, honeysweet through and through.
Keen-eyed Sisters, singing airily,

Looking warily
Every way,
Guard the apple night and day,
Lest one from the East come and take it away.

Now consider the following sentence:

But some two or three months ago I asked the hospitality and assistance of your columns to draw public and civic attention to the above position of affairs, and to the fact that the use of the Embankment, as a thoroughfare, was limited, and, in fact, almost prohibited, by the very bad and deterrent condition of the roadway at both ends of the portion from Chelsea to Westminister, the rest of the road being fairly good, of fine proportions, and easily capable of being made into a most splendid boulevard, for all ordinary traffic, as a motor road, in which respect it was dangerously impossible at parts, and as a typical drive or walk.

Fowler points out in his essay on rhythm that the writer of that passage produced a single sentence 114 words long without a single slip in grammar, and adds: "That so expert a syntactician should be rhythm-deaf is amazing."

How is rhythm defined? As Fowler puts it:

Rhythmic speech or writing is like waves of the sea, moving onward with alternating rise and fall, connected yet separate, like but different, suggestive of some law, too complex for analysis or statement, controlling the relations between wave and wave, waves and sea, phrase and phrase, phrases and speech. In other words, live speech, said or written, is rhythmic, and rhythmless speech is at the best dead. . . . A sentence or a passage is rhythmical if, when said aloud, it falls naturally into groups of words each well fitted by its length and intonation for its place in the whole and its relation to its neighbors. . . . For while rhythm does not mean counting syllables and measuring accent-intervals, it does mean so arranging the parts of your whole that each shall enhance, or at least not detract from, the general effect upon the ear.

Too complex for analysis, Fowler says about rhythm, and in truth there is very little, general statements to one side, that can be said to define it. One substantive clue may be found, though, in Tennyson's "The Song of the Three Sisters":

For the blossom unto threefold music bloweth;
Evermore it is born anew,
And the sap in threefold music floweth . . .

A quarter of a century later, Tennyson wrote a far more familiar poem, "The Charge of the Light Brigade." We all know:

Half a league, half a league,
Half a league onward . . .

. . . and:

Cannon to the right of them,
Cannon to the left of them,
Cannon in front of them . . .

. . . and:

Theirs not to make reply,
Theirs not to reason why,
Theirs but to do and die . . .

No secret to the rhythm he has created: he's talking in threes. Certainly not to the exclusion of other elements, but the most pronounced of all, the number three is used to help form the rhythm of speech. It's as simple as one-two-three, as basic as learning our ABC's, as universal as three wise men, three wishes, three guesses and three cheers; or Wynken, Blinken, and Nod; the *Niña*, the *Pinta*, the *Santa María*; the Father, the Son, and the Holy Spirit. The very word *trinity* means the state of being threefold, and its mysteries underlie the language as well. When a superb writer like Barbara Tuchman, the historian, can give us a sentence that says, "Montesquieu was what Oscar Wilde would have liked to have been if he had had more money, less talent and no humor," see how she uses threeness (*money . . . talent . . . humor*) to delight the ear. She might have used two ingredients, or four; indeed, if she used three every time the effect would be deadly. But the power of three is there, and good communicators know it and use it.

The second strongest number, for its contribution to rhythm, is two, which forms the basis for comparison or contrast, as in *the good news and the bad news* or *the sacred and profane*. Even there, threeness has its place: Lear had three daughters, one good, two bad; Cinderella was good, her two stepsisters were bad, and the prince tested the slipper three times.

That is as far as this analysis can go, because of the complexity of the subject. Fowler concludes his essay on rhythm by giving "a few examples of unrhythmical prose, followed by a single master-piece of rhythm. If these are read through several times, it will perhaps be found that the splendour of the last, and the meanness of the others, become more conspicuous at each repetition." He proceeds to give several awful examples, including the 114-word jobbie quoted above. Then the single masterpiece:

And the king was much moved, and went up to the chamber over the gate and wept: and as he wept, thus he said: O my son Absalom, my son, my son Absalom! Would God I had died for thee, O Absalom, my son, my son!

robber—see **burglar**

107

S

sarcastic—see *ironic*

sardonic—see *ironic*

satiric—see *ironic*

seasonable, seasonal *Seasonable* is opportune, occurring in good or proper time, suitable to the circumstances or season, and—sometimes—early. *Seasonal* is narrower, relating to a season in some specific way. Thus, *You will have to get to the market at a* seasonable *hour to get the pick of the corn and other* seasonal *crops.*

secondly—see *firstly*

sentinel, sentry Though dictionaries define a *sentinel* as *sentry*, they aren't quite the same. A *sentry* has more of a military, even belligerent, nature. A *sentinel* is friendlier; and lonelier too. We can imagine many sentries surrounding an encampment or installation, but sentinels come one to a location. And one other shade of difference: *sentries* exist for the well-being of those they surround or enclose. (*To protect those inside the camp, sentries were posted every 300 yards*); but *sentinels* serve outsiders and strangers as well (*For ships approaching the harbor, the lighthouse was a sentinel in the night*).

separate—see *divide*

seriously As in "But seriously, folks . . ." this word is like *frankly* or *honestly* in its potential to irritate the reader or listener. A light or humorous approach is often the right way to set out to request a favor or offer a criticism or observation. We then say, "Seriously . . ." or "But seriously . . ." to signal that we've now come to the point. But handle this with care. At times the *seriously* telegraphs that you thought there was a need to sugar-coat your statement or request. And too often, it implies that your reader or listener is so stupid he doesn't know when a joke is over. (It also helps if the joke, or other attempt at humor, was at least reasonably funny to begin with. It's noteworthy how many people lay a bomb, get no laugh, and then say, "But seriously . . .")

slogan—see **motto**

so—see **as**

solid, stolid   *Stolid* means impassive, and applies only to people (or an occasional basset hound). *Solid* has many meanings (none of them *stolid*) and can be applied to people, things, situations, as in a *solid citizen, a solid hunk of lead, a solid row of buildings, a solid meal.*

start—see **begin**

stationary, stationery   The stuff we write on is spelled with an *e*.

stimulant, stimulus   A *stimulant* is something that produces a *temporary* speeding up of some form of human or animal activity. The effect of a *stimulus* can be long lasting, and it can be applied to things and concepts as well as people and animals. So where ephedrine is a *stimulant* to a race horse, reduced interest rates can be a *stimulus* to the housing industry.

strategy, tactics   *Strategy* is the formulation of a plan; *tactics* are the way it's executed. See the earlier entry on **logic**: We would have to say Douglas was a splendid strategist but a lousy tactician.

subjunctive   In the first part of this book, the prediction appeared that phrases like *if I were king* may be on their way out, to be replaced in future usage by *if I was king*. In the first of these, the *were* reflects the use of the subjunctive mood, and it is being used less and less.

The subjunctive deals with concepts rather than facts. It is the mood of supposing, and most of the time it carries a negative assumption. Thus, when you say, "If I were king," you're saying, "Suppose I were king—though obviously I'm not, and never was." But a man who had in fact been a king, then abdicated his throne, could get away with saying, "If I was king," since in fact he already has been.

Some people not only use the subjunctive but abuse it. *Jones knew that if he were to become majority stockholder, he would have to enlist more backers* contains the subjunctive *were* instead of the indicative *was*, and is wrong for that reason. There is no automatic negative prospect in his becoming majority stockholder. There is a way for him to do that: get more backing. The supposition is there, but the essential negative is missing.

In the present tense, the subjunctive is concerned exclusively with concepts, regardless of whether any negative implication exists. *Jones asks that he be allowed to talk with his backers* gives us the subjunctive *be* (instead of the indicative *is*). *Jones is concerned that Smith give him his proxy* produces the subjunctive *give* (instead of the indicative *gives*).

The subtleties of the subjunctive are such that they are being learned—for that matter, being taught—by fewer and fewer people. One standard ballad, "If You Were the Only Girl in the World (and I Were the Only Boy)," employed the subjunctive correctly, but popular usage soon made it "I *Was*" instead of "I *Were*," and a comedian named Jackie Miles may have summed it up: "If you were the only girl in the world and I was the only boy, okay . . . but till then, forget it."

substantial—see **essential**

superlative degree—see **comparative**

surprise—see **amaze**

syntax—see **grammar**

T

tactics—see *strategy*

take place—see *occur*

talent—see *genius*

tangible—see *palpable*

thanking you in advance   Harry Shaw refers to this as "a hackneyed term in inferior business letters." Bergen and Cornelia Evans write, "Some people object to the phrase because it is ungrammatical and illogical, but these are only minor faults: it is insolent. To ask a favor and in the very act of asking it to state blandly that the person from whom the favor is begged need expect no thanks after it is done is so ludicrous that if it were not common, one would not believe that it had ever been done."

Actually, there *is* some logic to it, to the extent that *in advance* recognizes that the favor has not yet been performed; and thanking people beforehand is no automatic proof you don't intend to thank them afterwards as well. Nevertheless, both Shaw and the Evanses are right: regardless of whether the favor has yet occurred, the phrase presumes that it will, and so at best it's a gratuitous expression, and many letter recipients will be turned off by it.

How then should we say thank you in advance if we can't say "Thank you in advance"? The remedy lies in the realization that we don't have to wait till the favor is performed before we say "Thank you." The *in advance* is unnecessary.

We're still not completely in the clear, though. *Thank you* by itself, particularly in writing, where the typewriter, unlike the voice, can't convey any quality of warmth, can often seem abrupt, if not downright curt.

To the rescue, then, two more little words: *very much*. Put *thank you very much* in the place of *Thanking you in advance*, and you've warmed it up. The insolence is replaced by sincerity. Even the grammar is improved.

that, this   The plural forms are **those** for *that*, and **these** for *this*, and the issue of when to use which is usually governed by a basic rule: whatever is closer in time or location, or more understood in thought, takes *this/these*. Some examples:

This idea you had today is better than that idea you had yesterday. . . .

That pencil on the desk works better than this pencil in my hand. . . .

These people in our office are more fun to work with than those people in the office upstairs. . . .

Those thoughts (of yours) are no substitute for these (of mine).

Note in the last example that *these* is not followed by a noun, and the same can be true for *this, that* and *those.* In such cases they become what's called a "demonstrative pronoun," describing something referred to, but the same rule applies: *This is my wife I'm talking to on the phone.* . . . *Is that my wife you're talking to (on the phone)?* . . . *These are your shoes I'm wearing, those (in the closet) are mine.* Note there that *those* referred to your shoes, *these* to the shoes of the person you were talking to: it's the closer location of the shoes on your feet versus the ones in the closet, not the question of whose feet, that dictated the choice.

When there's no real difference on the basis of closeness, it's all right to mix and match. Say you have two bags of marbles on the table before you, and you point to each one in turn. *These are mine and those are my brother's* is fine, but so are *these . . . these, those . . . these,* or *those . . . those.*

You could also say, "Never bet on a gray horse: that (or *this*) is my advice to you." But reverse it, and you can only say, "*This* (not *that*) is my advice to you: Never bet on a gray horse," because here the word *advice,* which *this* is used to describe, is closer in point of time than the contents of that advice, which have yet to come. *This* takes the precedence of immediacy.

How many people can articulate this (or that) rule governing *this* and *that* is a question lacking any significance. Most people automatically select the right one, and that's it. The only problem arises when there's no real reason to choose one over the other. In such instances, as we've said, either will do, although (especially in writing), when the word has to follow the conjunction *that—Never bet on a gray horse: I believe that (this/that) is the best advice I can give*—some people prefer *this* because they shy away from the looks of *that that.* True, the conjunction can sometimes be omitted, but then the reader, accustomed to seeing the conjunction *that* follow *believe*, may have to stop to take bearings. There's nothing wrong with *that that*, if its use seems called for.

thing Some grammarians complain that this word is used so loosely that it has no real meaning, and they feel its use should be reserved only for those times when one has some specific object or entity in mind and then designates (or has already designated) the entity itself.

Yes, but one of the dictionary definitions of *thing* is "an object or entity not precisely designated or capable of being designated."

The trouble with *thing* is not that it can be applied loosely (if anything that's the chief purpose and strength of the word), but that it can be used too often. The thing of it is that things do have names, and without making a thing of it or doing inaccurate things or worrying about every single thing, it is possible, and commendable, to be precise about things, and why not? You can still do your own thing.

thirdly—see *firstly*

Tom Swifties The earlier section here on States Bates disease cautioned against the substitution of extra-explanatory verbs for *say/ said*. Equally bad is to use *said* but then modify it with some explanatory adverb. Well and good to substitute *said* for *consoled*, but if you make it *said consolingly*, what have you gained?

The point might be illustrated by a word game called "Tom Swifties," in vogue for a brief while during the 1960s, that involved both States Bates—the speaking verb placed ahead of the speaker— and the adverb modifying *said*: "*I want to be a hockey star*," *said Tom puckishly.* . . . "*Membership in this country club is restricted*," *said Tom waspishly.* . . . "*Those three inmates escaped by sliding down a rope outside the prison wall*," *said Tom condescendingly.*

"Do not explain too much," E. B. White has written. ". . . Let the conversation itself disclose the speaker's manner or condition. Dialogue heavily weighted with adverbs after the attributive verb is cluttery and annoying."

treachery, treason   They mean the same, but *treason* is used only for *treachery* against country. On the other hand, even a gin rummy hand can be treacherous.

try and/to   *Try* takes the infinitive. Probably another losing battle here, with all sorts of erudite types saying things like "Try and remember." Try and forget *try and remember* and make it *try* to *remember*—in fact, *try to* any verb—instead. Same rule applies to *go and/to*. *Go and see grandma* should be *Go to see grandma*. Or *Go see grandma* and forget it.

typical—see **average**

U

unilateral—see **bilateral**

uninterested—see **disinterested**

unique   There are no degrees of *unique*. No rather or mildly or somewhat or very or nearly or slightly or generally or partly or almost. If the word can't stand by itself, don't use it.

university—see **college**

unlawful—see **illegal**

unreadable—see **illegible**

unthinkable—see **inconceivable**

V

virtually—see **practically**

W

whatever, whatsoever Which one of the following is wrong?

A. *Whatever is wrong, is wrong.*

B. *Whatsoever is wrong, is wrong.*

C. *Whatsoever is right, is right.*

D. *Whatever is right, is right.*

Answer: Entry C, *Whatsoever is right, is right,* is wrong. The -*so*- is used to intensify a negative statement, not a positive one. Thus: *Any excuse whatever will suffice* is okay. So is *No excuse whatever/whatsoever will suffice.* But *Any excuse whatsoever will suffice* won't suffice.

In contrast to Americans, the English have a foolproof way of handling *whatsoever.* They don't use it at all.

when, where *When* is an expression of time, and *where* an expression of place, and both of them are often misused following the word *is* as a means of definition: *Public television is where you don't have commercials.* (Correct would be something like *Television without commercials is called public television.*) A *Dictionary of Contemporary American Usage* says, "*When* cannot be used to join a clause to a noun as children sometimes do in giving a definition, as in *intoxication is when you've had too much to drink,*" but this condemnation could as easily have included *where,* and why the violators are limited to the youth of the nation is a question. Senior citizens do it as much as anyone.

As to the time/place distinction, there are times where it's all right to ignore it, but this sentence is not one of them, any more than we can say there are places when it's also all right. *Times* has to take *when,* not *where;* and *places, where,* not *when.*

But in *There was a point early in her speech* when/where *she quoted Churchill*, either word is okay, because *point* can refer to either time or place.

whether Remarkably few people use this word by itself, although in many cases it can and should be used that way. Most people follow it with the word *or*—*Whether it rains or snows, we're still going. . . . I asked him whether he had eaten breakfast or not.* In the first example the *or* is necessary to connect *rain* with *snow*, but the *or not* in the second example is totally unnecessary. On the other hand, clarity is sometimes served by appending *or not*, and Roy Copperud writes, "Although some insist *or not* is redundant, the form is so well established they may as well turn their attention to weightier matters."

Copperud and others do point out, though, that using *as to* before *whether*—"the question as to whether he had dinner"—is a no-no.

wide—see **broad**

Y

yours truly A sign-off, and not just for this book. In the evolution of the language, *yours truly* became *yours very truly/very truly yours* in the expectation that the intensifier *very* would warm it up. It didn't. What happened was the opposite. Today, any letter we get from a lawyer, a bookkeeper, a collection agency, will close with *Very truly yours*—and the nastier and more threatening the contents, the greater the inevitability of that sign-off. It is, in short, the coldest, most formal closing we have, even when not so intended. One way to avoid it is to do just that—avoid it. Another is to take the original process and run it backwards: instead of putting in the *very* to warm it up, take the *very* out. *Yours truly/truly yours* are far gentler and warmer without it.

ABOUT THE AUTHOR

Charles Einstein has published more than five million words as newspaperman, columnist, editor, novelist, screenwriter and prize-winning author. He has written 34 books and more than 400 magazine articles and stories, with television credits ranging from Playhouse 90 to the Lou Grant Show; and three of his novels have become motion pictures, including the Fritz Lang classic *While the City Sleeps*. A winner of a Benjamin Franklin citation from the University of Illinois for magazine fiction, he is the author also of *Willie's Time*, the acclaimed biography of Willie Mays. His manuscripts and papers are housed in the Special Collections of the Boston University Libraries.

Catalog

If you are interested in a list of fine Paperback
books, covering a wide range of subjects
and interests, send your name and address,
requesting your free catalog, to:

McGraw-Hill Paperbacks
1221 Avenue of Americas
New York, N.Y. 10020

HOW TO COMMUNICATE
The Manning, Selvage & Lee Guide to Clear Writing and Speech

Charles Einstein

How to Communicate is a lively guide to style, clarity and precision from one of the world's largest public relations firms. Effective communication in this age of corporate gobbledygook and technocratese is essential — whether you're writing to your senator or landlord or working on a speech or a press release to your local newspaper.

A key to good communicating is writing for the ear as well as the eye. *How to Communicate* steers readers clear of the drowsy rhythms of deadpan business English. It includes a discussion on rules and when to break them, plus the real reason why *hopefully* is bad usage.

The second part of the book is a cross-referenced index of words, rules, subjects and phrases. Using examples of style, good and bad, from Casey Stengel to William Styron, this guide provides a lesson from the pros on the fine art of clear, persuasive writing.

Manning, Selvage & Lee is a full-service international public relations agency, one of the oldest and largest in the world. Founded in 1938, the firm is based in New York with major offices in 20 other cities across the U.S. and around the world. Author and former journalist Charles Einstein joined Manning, Selvage & Lee in 1981 as Senior Vice President and Editorial Director.

ISBN 0-07-039928-X